STRENGTH OF CONVICTION

TOM MULCAIR

STRENGTH OF CONVICTION

DUNDURN
A J. PATRICK BOYER BOOK

Project editor: Carrie Gleason
Editor: Michelle Tisseyre
Copy editor: Cy Strom
Cover designer: Grafikar
Interior design: Courtney Horner
Cover photographer: Michel Cloutier
Printer: Marquis

All family photographs unless otherwise noted © the Mulcair family and may not be reused without permission. Photos of the NDP © NDP Party and may not be reproduced without permission. Additional photographs are from the Quebec *Assemblée nationale* and are in the public domain.

Library and Archives Canada Cataloguing in Publication

Mulcair, Tom, 1954-, author
        Strength of conviction / Tom Mulcair

Includes index.
Issued in print and electronic formats.
ISBN 978-1-4597-3295-7 (paperback).--ISBN 978-1-4597-3296-4 (pdf).--
ISBN 978-1-4597-3297-1 (epub)

        1. Mulcair, Tom, 1954-. 2. Politicians--Canada--Biography. 3. New
Democratic Party--Biography. 4. Canada--Politics and government--
2006-. I. Title.

FC641.M84A3 2015   971.07'3092   C2015-904028-0
                                                                                    C2015-904029-9

1   2   3   4   5   19   18   17   16   15

We acknowledge the support of the **Canada Council for the Arts** and the **Ontario Arts Council** for our publishing program. We also acknowledge the financial support of the **Government of Canada** through the **Canada Book Fund** and **Livres Canada Books**, and the **Government of Ontario** through the **Ontario Book Publishing Tax Credit** and the **Ontario Media Development Corporation**.

Care has been taken to trace the ownership of copyright material used in this book. The author and the publisher welcome any information enabling them to rectify any references or credits in subsequent editions.
                                                                        — *J. Kirk Howard, President*

The publisher is not responsible for websites or their content unless they are owned by the publisher.

Printed and bound in Canada.

VISIT US AT
Dundurn.com | @dundurnpress | Facebook.com/dundurnpress | Pinterest.com/dundurnpress

Dundurn
3 Church Street, Suite 500
Toronto, Ontario, Canada
M5E 1M2

Contents

Foreword
by Ed Broadbent

S*trength of Conviction* is at once a biography, a behind the scenes look at an exciting period in our politics, and a blueprint for a stronger and more compassionate Canada.

In these pages Tom Mulcair makes a compelling case for change. Change, not only in the priorities we need to focus on to make life better for all Canadians, but in the tone of our politics.

I hope that Canadians, who now have the opportunity to choose a truly progressive government in Ottawa, come to know better the Tom Mulcair that I have gotten to know. Tom's upbringing shaped his values and principles. He was the second oldest of ten children in a middle-class household north of Montréal. Growing up in a full and lively house, Tom was encouraged by his parents to witness and participate in adult political discussion. His high-school teacher, Father Cox, taught him as a teenager that it was not only possible to rid the world of certain injustices, it was morally important to do so. Action, not simply talk, was what a good life should be all about.

The distinguished editor of *Le Devoir* and Québec Cabinet minister, Claude Ryan, mentored Tom in his early years in public service. Ryan taught his associates that, at its best, politics transcends mere compromise and embodies elements of pure justice.

And of course from Jack Layton, who brought Tom into the New Democratic Party as his Québec lieutenant, Tom learned unyielding optimism and Jack's own inspiring catchphrase: "Don't let them tell you it can't be done!"

But those who know Tom best know that of all the influences on Tom's life, that of his wife Catherine has been the greatest. If Tom's passion in politics comes through most vividly when he discusses the environment, his personal warmth comes through most strongly when his family and friends are in the picture. Catherine is his moral compass.

The one theme throughout Tom's impressive public life has been his determination to back his principles with action. He did so as a regulator defending patients who were abused by their doctors. He did so again when he resigned his Cabinet post as Québec's environment minister for refusing to permit condo developments on parkland. And most recently, he followed his principles with courageous action when he led the Opposition to the gross curtailment of civil liberties in the Conservative government's surveillance law, Bill C-51.

Tom Mulcair writes that he wants to build "a good and decent Canada where all can prosper, and no one is left behind." His strong stand on principle, in the tradition of the New Democratic Party and its past leaders, has brought the party within reach of this worthy goal.

— *Ed Broadbent*
Ottawa, 2015

Acknowledgements

Québec is where I grew up, spent a large part of my life, and have taken a number of very public positions throughout my career in government and provincial politics. For that reason Québecers got to know me, my character, my values, where I stand on issues, and whether what I say actually matches what I do.

In 2012, shortly after I was elected national leader of the NDP, Michelle Tisseyre, a Québec publisher and dear friend whom I first got to know during the 1995 referendum campaign and who shared my commitment to keeping our amazing country together, approached me about writing my life's story. I wasn't keen on the idea, because I've always believed in letting actions speak for themselves, and the whole "book thing" seemed like more self-glorification than I'd ever feel comfortable with. Not to mention that, as the newly elected leader of the Official Opposition, I was busier than ever.

Then last year, just before Christmas, Michelle's mother, whose name she shares, passed away, and Québec lost a famous radio and television personality going back to the early days of the CBC. Because I was unable to attend the funeral, I reached out to Michelle and invited her to lunch. Toward the end of the meal, with the persistence for which the Tisseyres are famous (I was in law school with one of her brothers), she asked me again whether I would consider writing my story and offered to publish it in French. Because Michelle is also a writer, I replied that if she wanted to, *she* could write the book. I'd give her access to all my archives and arrange for her to talk with the people I'd worked with. But she wasn't persuaded. It had to be *my* book. She suggested I write whenever I could, for instance on long flights as I travelled across Canada, and record the rest, perhaps with my wife Catherine, my sons Matt and Greg, and other close friends helping to jog my memory. She offered to help me edit what I produced, in both official languages.

Having accepted Michelle's kind offer to help me pull these many varied strands together, I am first and foremost indebted to her. If we were able to gather my recollections, reflections, and lessons learned and pull them into something resembling a full portrait, it is primarily thanks to her friendship, patience, and editorial skill. She's also one of the hardest workers I've ever met, which made it possible, despite a totally unrealistic schedule, to actually get the job done.

To my friends and colleagues who received endless fact-checking emails, my sincere gratitude. Chantale Turgeon, my deputy chief of staff in Ottawa, has been with me through thick and thin for over a decade and helped inform much of the discussion dealing with my time as environment minister. Ian Gillespie, who worked tirelessly and brilliantly throughout my leadership campaign, was of immeasurable assistance with research and narrative. I'd also like to thank Greg Yost for sharing his insight (and wry sense of humour).

With a packed schedule to contend with, much of my writing had to be done in transit. I thank BlackBerry Limited because I'm the only person I know who uses his BlackBerry as a laptop, tablet, and scrapbook.

Most importantly, I'd like to thank Catherine, Greg, Matt, and Matt's wife Jasmyne, each of whom, despite their own busy schedules, always managed to find time to read, propose, correct, and improve what I was writing. My close confidant and media assistant George Smith spent endless hours with Catherine and me poring over transcripts on our various trips around Canada; he deserves a medal of honour for his patience. Geoff Chambers, Brad Lavigne, and Alain Gaul have all contributed reminders, suggestions, and their collective keen eye for detail. Many thanks to each of them.

Finally, I'd like to thank my publishers, Michelle Tisseyre Éditeur and Dundurn Press, the largest independent, Canadian-owned book publishing company in the country. Dundurn's publisher, Kirk Howard, had known Michelle's late father Pierre, founder of Éditions Pierre Tisseyre, as well as François, Michelle's late brother who, as noted, was one of my friends in law school. So serendipity seemed to be at work from the beginning. I very much enjoyed writing this book and I hope Canadians enjoy reading it.

— *Tom Mulcair*
Stornoway, June 2015

Chapter One
Roots

My first Remembrance Day as the member of Parliament for Outremont will always stay with me. The year was 2007. I had just won a highly improbable victory in a by-election in the riding that had been a Liberal fortress almost continuously since its creation in 1935. I was the new federal MP, having represented my childhood home of Chomedey when I was in provincial politics. The ceremony began beneath a cold November sky. The war memorial that stands in Outremont Park is a white marble slab, marked with the names of the fallen in the First and Second World Wars on its back and sides. The monument's most arresting feature is an allegorical bronze sculpture that sits in the foreground, representing the town of Outremont as a mother grieving over the death of her sons. Standing in that place, it is impossible not to feel intense gratitude toward the brave Canadians who gave their lives to help make Canada what it has become. Laying the ceremonial wreath that day on behalf of my constituents was for me a deeply meaningful act. It spoke not only to my responsibility as a representative of the people of the riding, but to something much more personal as well. Both my mom and my dad had lived in Outremont as children. My dad, who along with his twin brother Bobby was the youngest in a family of nine, had seen two of his older brothers go off to the war. Only one had come back. The other, a pilot in the Royal Canadian

Air Force, had been killed during training before leaving for the front. His name, like mine, was Thomas Mulcair. After the ceremony I walked around the side of the monument and looked for my uncle's name among the list of Second World War dead. The French and English names were grouped under the different services. I scanned those listed under "Aviation — Air Force," and suddenly there he was: T.C. Mulcair. I felt a chill run through my body in that cold November wind, but also a deep sense of humility. I was filled with thoughts of the sacrifice that this man had made for our country — and a sense of duty to at least try to live up to the contribution he, and others in my family, had made, in that time and before. You'd never have guessed it from the modest, middle-class town where my brothers and sisters and I were brought up, Laval, Québec — my parents struggling to pay the bills and raise ten kids — but our family roots stretch back to Canada's very beginnings, including one of the oldest and proudest political dynasties in Canada.

My dad's family was from classic, hard-spun Irish Catholic roots. His grandfather, my great-grandfather, had been born near the Mulcair River in County Limerick, Ireland, and had emigrated to Canada during the Great Irish Famine of the 1840s. My dad's dad, like my uncle whose name is inscribed on the memorial in Outremont, was Thomas Mulcair. My own dad was Henry Donnelly Mulcair. His mother was a Donnelly, so he was as Irish as you can get.

My dad had eight brothers and sisters growing up — a big Irish Catholic family, just like the one he had with my mom later in life. The last of Dad's siblings to pass was his sister, my Auntie Evelyn. Aunt Evelyn had never married. During our last conversation, three years ago, as she lay dying in St. Mary's Hospital in Montréal, she asked me whether I had ever been to the memorial in the park in Outremont. Of course I had, I said. I had seen the name of her brother Tom inscribed there in the stone. She explained that unlike my grandfather and me, he was Thomas Cornelius and not Thomas Joseph. Then she managed one of her beautiful smiles and said that he'd always hated that middle name. That was when she told me something far more serious, that no one else in the family had ever mentioned. There was another name on that memorial, she said, the name of a boy she'd been in love with before he went off to the war. He never came back, either, and she'd never fallen in love again. She told me his name, and the next time I went, there it was. It touched me deeply.

My mom, Jeanne Hurtubise, grew up in a French-Canadian Catholic family of nine, just like Dad. My mother and father's family story is full of such coincidences, but, in other ways, their backgrounds couldn't have been more different. My mom's ancestors on her mother's side were French, going all the way back to the creation of New France. The first of them to come to these shores was Julien Mercier, who hailed from Tourouvre, in Perche, and was one of the colony's earliest settlers, arriving from France in the mid-1600s. One of his descendants was Honoré Mercier, Mom's great-grandfather, who was premier of Québec from 1887 to 1891. The Mercier Bridge, along with two electoral ridings in Montréal, one federal and one provincial, are named after him. As a young lawyer he had been opposed to the Confederation project, fearing that it would disadvantage French-Canadians and endanger the survival of the French language. Nevertheless, by 1872 the agreement reached by the Fathers of Confederation had allayed his fears to the point where he ran for Parliament in the riding of Rouville and was elected to the House of Commons. Mercier later helped found the Québec Liberal Party and was elected to the Québec Legislative Assembly in the riding of Saint-Hyacinthe in 1879, becoming leader of his party in 1883. Mercier continued to practise law while in office and, as president of the Québec Bar in 1885, strongly opposed the execution of Louis Riel. (According to family oral tradition, he and a group of French-Canadian business people helped take care of Riel's children after his death.) The hanging of Riel by Sir John A. Macdonald's government caused such discontent in Québec that the province became a political wasteland for the Conservative Party for the better part of a century. Premier Honoré Mercier is remembered as an advocate of more autonomy for the provinces, but also a champion of greater co-operation. He was the first provincial premier to promote the idea of federal-provincial conferences. While visiting the Yukon in 2014, I got to see how far the branches of the Mercier family tree had reached. Paul Mercier, Honoré's son and Mom's grandfather, was an engineer who opened up the road to the Yukon in the early years of the Gold Rush. Paul met his wife, Marie-Louise Taché, in Whitehorse, which now has a thriving francophone community. They married in 1901 and theirs was one of the first non-indigenous weddings performed in the territory. Photographs of their wedding still hang in the francophone centre there. Paul Mercier's sister, Éliza Mercier, married Louie

Gouin, who was premier of Québec from 1905 to 1920 and later the federal member of Parliament for what is now the current riding of Outremont (then called Laurier–Outremont). Mom is also descended, on her father's side, from a third premier of Québec, the first to take office after Confederation: Pierre-Joseph-Olivier Chauveau, who was a Conservative. His son Pierre Chauveau married Martha Meagher, daughter of John Meagher, who was the federal MP for Gaspé of his day. Mom's Irish roots are just one more coincidence in my parents' story. So I have the Irish not only from the Mulcairs and Donnellys on my dad's side, but from the Meaghers on my mom's side as well. When we were growing up we knew family history and it meant a great deal to us, but by the time my siblings and I were born, it was just that — history. My mother and father both had to work very hard for everything they achieved in life, and they taught us to do the same. Mom received a good education at Villa Maria, a bilingual all-girls school in Notre-Dame-de-Grâce (N.D.G.), run by the nuns of the Congregation of Notre-Dame. She met Dad in Sainte-Anne-des-Lacs in the Laurentians when they were both sixteen. Theirs was a love at first sight, and they decided then and there to spend the rest of their lives together. By then both of their families had moved from Outremont to N.D.G. (another coincidence), so they were inseparable right from the start. Dad, who was attending Loyola High School, spoke fluent French, in part thanks to his mom, Irene Donnelly, who'd gone to a French convent and was fluently bilingual. His French got even better after meeting Mom and hanging out with her French-speaking friends.

My parents adored each other. They had ten kids, not by chance or by accident, as one might think, but by choice. Every time my mom gave birth, my dad would bring her fourteen roses, because they'd initially decided when they got married that they were going to have fourteen children. They stopped at ten, which, if you can believe it, led to a conflict with our parish priest (more on that a little later). When they were first married, they lived in a small apartment in a town called Wrightville, now part of Gatineau. I was born seventeen months after my elder sister Colleen, at Ottawa Civic Hospital, on the Ontario side of the Ottawa River. Shortly after, our parents took us to live in Ottawa, in a row house on St. Laurent Boulevard. Three years later they decided to move back to Montréal, to a house on Westmore Avenue, in N.D.G., where we all lived until I was four. By then Colleen and

I had three little brothers and sisters: Peter, Jeannie, and Danny. Mom was expecting our sister Deb when we moved again, for the third time in five years, and settled in Chomedey, a small town on what was then called Île Jésus, an island just on the other side of the bridge from Montréal, now called Laval. Today Laval is a vast and busy suburb of Montréal, but it was mostly fields back then. Our parents bought a house on 99th Avenue with three bedrooms, eventually adding two more rooms after they finished the basement. So many families were moving to Laval in those days that our small town quickly became a typical suburban neighbourhood, with flocks of kids running in the streets and a big park right across from our house where we played every day. We were into sports, lots of sports. We played baseball, football, and in winter — what else? — hockey, on the open-air rinks that are so much a part of the Canadian landscape.

Chomedey was, and has remained, a very mixed, linguistically and culturally diverse, suburban enclave. At that time, there was a large Greek community starting to form; a large Armenian community that was just moving in; a large English-speaking Jewish community with several synagogues; and one English Catholic church called Holy Name where we all went as a family. There was a lovely convent close to where we lived, where Mom used to take those of us who'd already had our First Communion for six o'clock mass once or twice a week, and sometimes as often as five days in a row. Our parents shared a deep religious faith. Like most Catholic families in Québec in the 1960s, we used to say the rosary together as a family before going to bed at night. Mom still remembers that when she first started going out with Dad, at sixteen, he told her his father said the rosary in Gaelic every night. Dad and his twin brother Bobby would start mimicking him. The more they mimicked him, the more slowly he would speak the Gaelic, adding more decades to his rosary and putting an end to their shenanigans pretty quickly.

In a large family, as anyone who was raised in one can attest, you learn your responsibilities early. The older children help to bring up the younger ones. In our family that role naturally fell to my sister Colleen and me. She and I were seventeen months apart and worked as a team to look after the newest baby, help our younger siblings with homework, and generally keep a close eye on our brothers and sisters. By the time Colleen and I were eight and nine, we had two more little sisters, Sheilagh and Maureen, who were still in diapers (Kelly rounded out the girls' squad and Sean, the youngest, was two when I started law school). I knew how to change a diaper, and did, many times a day — the cotton kind that you fastened with big safety pins. There were no disposables, and in any case, new parents today know all too well how expensive those are. Today cloth diapers are making a comeback, thanks to environmentally conscious young entrepreneurs whose diaper service companies offer a less expensive, more sustainable product for the benefit of today's busy, cash-strapped parents.

As we grew older Colleen and I took on more responsibility. Our duties included all the household chores. Dad was a very good role model. He not only changed diapers and took care of the smaller kids, but he was a very good cook, and always cleaned up in the kitchen after meals. By the time Colleen and I were eleven and twelve we babysat whenever our parents had to go out. In the early years Mom stayed home practically all the time; on that subject, one of my constituents told me a story, much later, when I became the member of the *Assemblée nationale* for Chomedey. Thelma Comire, who had been a neighbour of ours back then and one of "the grown-ups" we knew as children, recalled how, whenever there were several moms standing outside chatting, and any one of my brothers or sisters came up to ask Mom something, she would just put her hand up to her friends and say, "Excuse me for a second." Then she would crouch down, listen to what her child had to say and take care of whatever it was, before returning to the conversation. That small gesture, which Mrs. Comire remembered so well, was something I'd never really thought about, because to us it was just normal. That was our mom. In her eyes, we were always number one. Looking back, I can see just how lucky we were.

As the family grew, money also grew tight. With eleven of us in the house — eventually twelve — we needed all hands on deck. By the time I was fourteen, Mom had already started teaching, first as a substitute, and after a few months basically full-time, at Sacred Heart Elementary School in Chomedey. That was the school we went to as children and where, in the winter months, the mothers would get called to come and shovel the snow off the roof. Because the building was prefabricated and made of plywood, after every snowfall the roof was in danger of collapsing. At recess the kids would watch the moms walk up the snowbanks that met the roof and start shovelling — which is hard work, if you've ever done it. Our education was in English but, as our school belonged to a Catholic school board where the majority of schools were French, ours was in the minority and underfunded: hence the plywood. Initially the building had been put up as a temporary structure, but it served for many years before a permanent one replaced it.

As Dad was fluently bilingual, in our early years in Chomedey he had a good job as a regional manager for l'Industrielle, a Québec City insurance company that at the time was called Industrial Life. The company's president, Jean-Louis Lévesque, also owned the Blue Bonnets race track and helped found the Montréal Heart Institute. Dad ran the Montréal office and often had business in Québec City, so for us kids a big getaway treat was to be taken along in the back seat of his car. Dad left l'Industrielle just at the end of the sixties to go to work for Armstrong and Taylor, another insurance outfit based in western Canada, eventually becoming vice-president. Nevertheless, with a family our size, money was always tight. When I was in grade seven I wrote the entrance exams for Loyola High School, which Dad and his twin brother Bobby had attended. He was really proud when I was accepted, though I was a bit more ambivalent, because I knew it would be an extremely long commute to get there from Laval every day. Then, one day, sometime before the end of the school year, I remember Dad calling me up to my parents' bedroom. He looked uncharacteristically sad. He simply said, "Look, Tommy, I've seen what it'll cost to send you to Loyola, and with eight other kids to feed, we just can't afford it right now. I promise you that when it comes time to go to university, we'll be able to help pay for whichever one you might want to go to." I was secretly relieved, because there was another downside to Loyola: no girls.

In the spring of 1973 Armstrong and Taylor was sold to an American company. Many of the Canadian executives were let go, including Dad. He was now unemployed, in his early forties, with no severance, ten kids still at home, and very tough prospects. What he did next shows the mettle of the man. Our family had a cottage up north, on Lac Marois in Sainte-Anne-des-Lacs. Mom's father, Pierre Hurtubise, had a large chicken farm in the village and had been its first mayor. My parents had gotten married in the village church. It was just a summer cottage, with no heating, nothing beyond the most basic amenities. Early that spring Dad began going up there to study toward obtaining a licence as a general insurance broker. He'd been handed a raw deal but he wasn't going to take it. Dad vowed he would never put his family's fate in someone else's hands again. I can still hear him saying he'd never wear a tie to work again … but in much more colourful and unprintable terms.

After Dad got his broker's licence he opened an office in Montréal and started building up his business. Then he sold the house, moved our family up north, and opened an office there. We survived, but times were really tough. Mom had experience teaching at Sacred Heart, so she very quickly found a teaching job to help support the household. She later taught at Boys' Farm, a reform school for young offenders and troubled teens that's now called Shawbridge Youth Centres, in the village of Shawbridge in the Laurentians. We kids used to joke that raising us had prepared her for a job in a reform school. She loved working there.

Needless to say, when we were growing up none of us had much of an allowance. There were just too many of us, and our parents couldn't afford it. If we wanted something we had to earn the money ourselves. I had my first paper route when I was ten, delivering the *Montreal Star* to homes around Chomedey, and my second when I was twelve, delivering the *Gazette*. As kids, when one of us needed money to buy something, we used to help each other out. My younger sister Jeannie, who is three years younger than me, reminded me recently of a good turn I'd done her when she was starting high school. She needed penny loafers, the casual slip-ons that were all the rage that year, and of course when she asked Mom and Dad for money to buy them, they said, "No, you've already got shoes, you don't get other shoes." I bought her the penny loafers with money from my paper route. I was still delivering papers in my first year of CÉGEP at Vanier College (CÉGEP is the Québec equivalent of what used to be called junior college).

Even if money was always tight, times were good for us growing up. When we lived in Chomedey, we would go up north in the summer and spend our time exploring the woods and swimming in the lake. We were all good swimmers, and I later competed on the swim team at Vanier College. In the winter we used to go up there on weekends to ski. Of course, like all kids in Québec, I was a rabid Habs fan and never missed a game on television. Dad often refereed the outdoor hockey games that took place in the park across our street. He knew all the rules — and not just the rules of hockey. It got to the point where in summer the kids playing football in the park would come running to consult him, because he knew all the rules of football, too.

Dad had been a serious hockey player (he'd played for the Junior Canadiens) and, as a result, he was sometimes given hockey tickets. One day when I was ten, he was offered a really good pair of seats and he invited me to go with him to the game. That was, hands down, the biggest event in my life until then. Because we were such a crew I didn't get much face time with my dad, so this was just amazing. On the night of the game I was so nervous I couldn't eat my dinner. We got to the Forum, the hallowed *temple du hockey*, where the Montreal Canadiens were going to play against — it couldn't get any better than this — the Toronto Maple Leafs. The competition between the two teams was so fierce in those years, it was already being called the greatest rivalry in hockey.

Once inside the arena we were treated to a surprise. In the years leading up to Expo 67 we kept hearing a string of fantastic things that were on the horizon for our city. We were going to get a subway. We were going to get a stadium. We were going to get a new boulevard that would cross the island of Montréal from one end to the other. As we went in to take our seats, there was an announcement on the PA system, informing the fans that we were about to get a peek at a high-tech wonder that was going to be filming some footage for the Bell pavilion at Expo 67. Sure enough, moments later a bunch of movie cameras, arrayed in a massive circular cluster, were lowered from the rafters high above our heads to hover just above centre ice, where they remained for the game. Three years later, when I visited the Bell pavilion at Expo 67, it featured a 360-degree movie projection that included the famous Musical Ride and, lo and behold, scenes from *that* hockey game, the one I'd been to with my dad. Watching a game with my dad was an education, but one of the rituals I witnessed that night needed no explanation. The Forum had its own long-established hockey traditions. Every time the Canadiens scored, hundreds of black galoshes would rain down on the ice (and for a hat-trick goal, scores of cheering fans would similarly lose their hats), all of which had to be removed with shovels before the match could continue.

As if going with Dad to see a real, live Canadiens game wasn't enough, what came next was the biggest thing to ever happen in Chomedey, as far as I was concerned: the Rocket, the great, the one and only Maurice Richard came to a nearby bowling alley, and my dad took me to meet him. I was so awestruck I couldn't speak, so Dad asked for his autograph instead of me. Richard was my idol and I loved playing hockey, but I sure wasn't headed for the NHL. The first year I played, Dad tried to coach me. He kept telling me to pick up the puck, but I could barely stand on my skates. I remember years later, one morning at breakfast, he told me about a dream he'd had of me playing hockey in Maple Leaf Gardens. We both laughed and thought no more about it. Yet forty years later, some colleagues and I who played on the *Assemblée nationale* hockey team went to Toronto to play a friendly game against a team of members of the Provincial Legislature. The game was played in Maple Leaf Gardens. Dad would have gotten such a kick out of seeing it.

My first summer job, in 1969 when I was fourteen, was working in a clothing factory for a buck twenty-five an hour, in the *schmatte* district of Montréal. There were other kids there my own age, but as the summer dragged on I realized that in September I was going back to school and they weren't. They were going to stay in that factory to help their families put food on the table. In my last year of CÉGEP and afterward in law school, I worked for four years in construction, doing tar and gravel roofs, which you'll know is hard work if you've ever done it — it kept me very fit. For me, those jobs were a way to earn money and pay my way through school. For most of the people I worked with, those jobs were their life. I remember one night coming home from work and telling Dad about hardships I'd heard the guys talking about that day. "Yeah," my dad said, "you're learning there are really two worlds out there."

While the workplace was where I was to witness the reality of these two worlds, it was at school that I first was made aware of their existence and began to sort out what I thought of them — and what I wanted to do about it. The year was 1968, my second at Chomedey High. The Vietnam War was at its height. On college and university campuses throughout Canada, the U.S., and Europe, student sit-ins and occupations were commonplace. In our school, the most revolutionary change was that religion classes had been replaced by an ethics course. It seemed like a small step forward compared to what was happening all around us in those tumultuous times, but the course turned out to be engaging and interesting. Our teacher was an American draft dodger with a unique perspective on the world we lived in.

Our high school had a very strict regimen, but one day my classmate John McMaster and I and some other kids boldly led a walkout to challenge what we saw as a grave injustice. We marched down to the basement of the annex building where the grade eight and nine classrooms were located. Then we staged a sit-in and refused to go back to our books until this outrage had been rectified. The school had taken away our recess, for whatever reason, and we weren't going to stand for it. Much to our surprise and satisfaction, our sit-in worked. The administration caved and reversed its decision, and we got our recess back. It was amid this heady atmosphere of student empowerment that we learned a new instructor was coming to teach some of our second year classes — a Catholic priest. A priest? In high school? It seemed like a step backwards. We were completely unprepared for the social and intellectual whirlwind that was about to hit us in the form of Father Alan Cox.

Father Alan Cox was in his early thirties and had already distinguished himself by working with the police to help street kids in Montréal. He had known Father Emmett Johns, who was called "Pops" on downtown streets, since the 1960s, and was cut from the same cloth. In those days they were both working with runaways and drug-addicted kids downtown, long before Johns would eventually establish *Le Bon Dieu dans la Rue* (now simply called *Dans la Rue*), a renowned charitable organization helping homeless youth. Father Cox's transfer to Laval was a godsend for me, but it wasn't until much later that I learned the real reason he had been sent there. Father Cox had been forced to come to Chomedey after the archdiocese declared that his ministering to street kids was unbecoming of a man of the cloth. For caring for the least among us, Father Cox was, quite literally, banished from the city to what the archdiocese probably hoped would be a quiet tenure in a sleepy, suburban parish. They would have no such luck.

When the decision had come down from the archdiocese to move Father Cox, he had been working in LaSalle, where an explosion and a fire in an apartment building had killed dozens of people. Father Cox had been working with the police and firemen to help the traumatized survivors, most of whom were poor and without insurance, to deal with the aftermath. When the archdiocese had first directed him to go to Laval he'd wanted nothing to do with it, but in the end he reconciled himself to the prospect and did what he was asked. What was a difficult time for Father Cox became a life-changing event for me. He arrived at our school in a vehicle that became known ever after as "the Coxmobile." Because he was very close to both the Montréal fire service, as a result of his help with survivors of the LaSalle disaster and of his chaplaincy work, and the police force, for his work with young people in conflict with the law, in order to thank him and to facilitate their continued work together, he'd been given an unmarked patrol car as his personal vehicle. It was replete with two-way radio and had the muscle-car engine of the Chrysler products of that era (it was a Dodge). Needless to say, we were suitably impressed.

Father Cox was a brilliant, tough, and extraordinarily determined teacher, and he had an equally tough message for us, his students: "Get off your duffs and learn to play a positive role in society. There's a lot of injustice out there that you need to be aware of. What's more, you need to do something about it." His message was grounded in the Gospel and the message of Jesus Christ, especially the Sermon on the Mount, but also anchored in the modern world. This was completely new to us, who'd grown up in a place where the Church reigned supreme and Mass — until recently — had been conducted exclusively in Latin. When Father Cox began saying Mass at our school, instead of finding any excuse not to attend, students started showing up in droves.

His homilies were calls to action. Father Cox challenged us. He inspired us. Sometimes he drove us nuts. He had what's called a vocation, especially for working with young people. We formed a youth group, which we called Paladin. When we met in the evenings, Father Cox would show us a film — for example, about motorcycle gangs — and then have a conversation with us, inviting us to express our opinions and debate what we'd seen. That kind of critical thinking wasn't part of the curriculum in many schools in those days, but Father Cox insisted on it. If Father Cox sensed that a student was telling him something because he thought it was what he wanted to hear, he didn't like it. At times he chided us for being part of a generation whose minds were going to mush from watching too much television. At other times he spoke with such hope for us all. He encouraged us to learn about the world, to read voraciously — he was incredibly well read — to get involved and make a difference in what was going on around us.

The year before, while he was still teaching in LaSalle, he'd organized a trip to Europe for the students in his charge. He wanted to do the same for our high school. It all sounds easy now. A trip to Europe — big deal, you might say. But in those days, for us, a bunch of wet-behind-the-ears fourteen-year-olds who'd never been more than fifty kilometres from our quiet suburban homes, it was unimaginably bold, adventurous, unheard of. Father Cox wanted us to understand what a big, wide world we were a part of.

For our parents, the trip was such a daunting prospect that it required many meetings at the school and individual visits by Father Cox to convince them to let us go. He sat down with Mom and Dad and explained what the trip was about, adding that the only requirement was that we get summer jobs and earn the money to pay for it. My parents were very open-minded, and Dad, who was particularly hard to impress, took an immediate shine to Father Cox; he especially approved of the condition that I come up with the money to pay for the trip. Recently, Alain Godbout, one of my high-school classmates on that trip, gave me his own copy of the original brochure that Father Cox had run off for our parents, showing the itinerary and the cost of the trip. When I opened it I couldn't believe my eyes. Our airfares for two transatlantic flights and eight more within Europe came to a grand total of $282. Thank you, Alain, for that priceless gift, and for holding onto it all these years.

Our group landed in Lisbon, Portugal, where, jet-lagged as we were after our all-night flight from Canada, we immediately got on a train for Fatima. There we walked all day and were received at a convent for a meal that our very Canadian palates found exotic beyond belief. It included a fish with its tail in its mouth on each of our plates. We were even allowed a small glass of wine. The group went back to our hotel, which surprisingly was called York House, where we were bunked four or six to a room and thought that it was the lap of luxury. We were on cloud nine, unaware that our trip was about to be marred by tragedy.

Early the next morning, after our first night in Fatima, we were woken up and asked to go immediately downstairs for a meeting. We quickly got up and were taken to a room, wondering what this was about. Father Cox came in. He didn't look well at all; the other adults looked miserable. Something was terribly wrong, but we couldn't imagine what it could be. Father Cox spoke. The night before, while hanging clothes on a line outside his window, Gary, one of our classmates, had slipped and fallen out of the window, hitting some wires on the way down. He had been killed instantly.

We had been through a year where Father Cox would often challenge our ability to think on our feet, to see how we'd react. So at first this just seemed to me as though it might be some extreme version of the same thing. Obviously, Gary would soon come walking through the door. But the tears streaming down Father Cox's face showed this wasn't a test. This was for real. Gary and I had worked in adjoining factories in Montréal's needle trade district that summer and had often eaten our lunches together by the railroad tracks at the back of the building. He'd lost a lot of weight working and was in great spirits as the trip began. Gary was a top student and an only child. We were just stunned and at a complete loss as to what to do.

Today, were such a tragedy to happen on a school trip, it would likely be cancelled — kids sent home to be with family and receive grief counselling. But this was a different time. When we discussed the matter with Father Cox and the other adults present, we voted to go back home. But it was the school principal, Mr. Lemieux, and our parents who made the call. We should continue the trip. There were more discussions and we all pitched in so the requisite seats could be purchased to have Gary's casket sent home. We remained in a collective state of shock for days but were encouraged to talk about how we felt, which, in retrospect, made us able to cope. And Father Cox was there for each of us, every step of the way.

We soon left Portugal, travelling to several countries, including Austria, where we stayed with a wonderful family that ran an old-style German tavern and inn, or *gasthaus,* called Hochsteg. It was in the town of Mayrhofen, in the Zillertal region — a majestic, awe-inspiring place. There was a minuscule Catholic church, and Father Cox, of course, said Mass there, just as he did on mountaintops at other random moments of the trip. The Eucharist had real meaning when said through him and, of course, Gary was always at the forefront of our thoughts. For us, it was a place of healing. Many years later, in 1990, I took my sons Matt and Greg to Mayrhofen. Catherine and I visited there in 2005. Matt and his wife Jasmyne included it in the itinerary for their honeymoon a couple of years later.

We travelled on to Yugoslavia, which at the time was slightly controversial. The country was still governed by a communist regime under Marshal Josip Broz Tito, who sought to maintain a measure of independence from the Kremlin. We were greatly amused by the men in dark suits and fedoras who wore bulky overcoats even though it was summer and who followed us everywhere. We took great glee in taking pictures of them.

Father Cox also took us to East Berlin. We went through Checkpoint Charlie — the most famous crossing through the Berlin Wall, featured in more than a few classic spy movies. On the way back, Danny Shkuda, who was a diabetic, felt faint and began to pass out. We had to literally carry him past screaming, machine-gun-wielding soldiers, until we were safely back on the West German side. When Father Cox passed away in November 2013 I had the honour of delivering the eulogy. When I mentioned this event, Danny came up and reintroduced himself forty-four years later. He was none the worse for wear.

The most unforgettable and revelatory part of the trip was the visit to the Dachau concentration camp. Located near Munich, it has been kept as an ugly reminder of the abject horror of the Nazi regime. We went through the camp in total silence. There was a group of nuns who prayed there full-time, literally around the clock, begging God for forgiveness. In later years this changed (a similar practice at Auschwitz caused controversy and was abolished ahead of the fiftieth anniversary of the Warsaw Ghetto uprising in April 1993), but, at the time, it seemed to make sense to seek atonement on the very site where these horrors had been perpetrated.

Walking through this place where countless human beings had been held and slaughtered, not for anything they'd done or who they were as individuals, but because of the people to which they belonged, left me deeply shaken. The realization I came to in that place has stayed with me ever since.

In the decades that have passed since those horrible crimes, peoples around the world have come to acknowledge, in many forms, that we have a collective responsibility to ensure that such a thing never, ever happens again — not to Jews, or anyone else. But the talks we had that day, with Father Cox as our guide, have always left me with the sincere belief that that responsibility falls on each and every one of us as individuals, as well. Father Cox was a mentor to me and one of the most profound influences in my life. In our youth group, what he was trying to make us understand was that there was an awful lot that was wrong in the world and that it was up to us to change it.

Although the summer wasn't over, when we returned from Europe we found our lessons were just beginning. Father Cox didn't let up. He got us involved in community service in Montréal. We'd get on the bus in Laval and ride up to Henri Bourassa Boulevard, and then take the Metro to one of the poorer neighbourhoods downtown. When we arrived, the local parish priest would be waiting for us and tell us where we were needed, for instance to help an elderly woman to move some furniture. The goal was to make us see the urgency of doing, as opposed to just talking, and to impress on us the idea that we could, that it was possible to get things done, to make a difference in people's lives. It's a lesson I've carried with me and that has guided me my whole life.

Nearly twenty years later, in 1988, when Father Cox learned that Mother Teresa of Calcutta would be visiting Canada, he wrote to her explaining the work he'd been doing with Catholic youth in Canada for a generation. She wrote back that she wanted to meet him and asked if it would be possible to come to Laval Catholic High School (at the time, the brand new regional high school) to meet with the students, learn about their lives, and share her life's work with them. Father Cox loved telling the story of how he'd kept the visit secret and, on the day of the visit, simply asked that all the students be brought down to the auditorium. He laughed as he explained their typical reaction: What was he up to this time? When they were assembled he walked to the centre of the stage, spoke simply, and told the students that Mother Teresa of Calcutta was there to speak with them. Total silence descended on the room as the diminutive saint moved to the microphone, where she held her young audience rapt.

The year 1969 was also the year I decided I was going to go into politics one day. Father Cox urged us to act — to get things done — and it seemed to me that political action was the best way to do it for a significant number of people. Politics was something I'd always talked about with our parents. Mom, after all, had politics in her blood, and both she and Dad were very progressive in their thinking. Growing up in such a large family, we didn't get a lot of face time with our parents, so at night around the dinner table, whenever they talked about politics, Colleen and I, and later the other children as they grew up, were encouraged to join in the discussion.

Our mother and father were both very respectful of other people's religions and of other cultures. In Québec this is very much in the freethinking, anticlerical, anti-establishment tradition of the nineteenth-century Liberal Party, and it is so much a part of my mother's heritage. As a matter of fact, our church attendance declined precipitously as a result of what happened after Mom and Dad decided not to have any more kids. This choice did not go down well with our parish priest, who refused to give Mom absolution when she said that she was using birth control. Mom and Dad were equally upset about that. No priest was going to tell Mom she had to have more children. Up until that summer we'd never been allowed to miss Mass, but from then on it became completely optional, as much for our parents as for any of us.

On the subject of politics my father could be ferocious — he cut through bullshit like no one I knew. His political antennae were very finely tuned. I can remember him watching televised coverage of the new budget once, when I was very young, probably at the time of Premier Daniel Johnson *père,* who was the leader of the conservative Union Nationale. The Union government was rolling back tax incentives that helped large families — a culturally significant measure in heavily Catholic Québec. Suddenly Dad threw his hands up and said, "Do you believe it? We won't be getting the deduction for the kids anymore! I might as well move to Ontario!" Of course, he never did.

Years later, when I was still in high school, I remember Dad coming back from Toronto after a luncheon at one of the major service clubs and talking to me about a man who had made a deep impression on him that day. "French guy was giving the speech," he said. "Name of Claude Ryan, Irish name. Very good. Very, very smart. Talking to them up there, saying, 'You have to listen to the Frenchmen, you have to understand what they're saying. There's some very different things going on in Québec. You can't just slam the door and ignore them.' Very impressive guy. Very courageous. Very important speech." That stayed with me because Dad, as a rule, was very hard to impress. It must have been the early 1970s, probably in the wake of the October Crisis, and this guy Ryan was telling that influential group of business leaders in Toronto that if they didn't listen, if they didn't get it, if they didn't understand that they had to accommodate their French-speaking fellow citizens, Canada itself could be lost. Not mincing words, telling it like it is — that way of giving it to you straight, as I would later discover, was so typical of Claude Ryan.

Dad didn't realize then what an impact his words would have on my life, as Claude Ryan, a provincial Liberal Cabinet minister, would eventually become my boss in the public service and the next important mentor in my life. Even if Dad could have realized how my path and Ryan's would cross in years to come, he would not have tried to influence my decisions based on his own personal opinion. That was one of the remarkable things about my parents and how they raised us: they guided us but didn't push us — in fact, just the opposite. One of the rare times my father did push me, though, was when I told him that I wanted to go to law school. Right off the bat he insisted that I study law in French. Up until then I had done all my schooling — elementary, high school, and CÉGEP — entirely in English. My French was competent for everyday use but grammatically inadequate, and given all the written work involved, I didn't see how I could do it. I was eighteen years old and I'd been accepted into McGill Law School directly from CÉGEP. The McGill Faculty of Law was one of the best in the world, and getting through it was going to be daunting. Switching to the Université de Montréal in order to study in French seemed an insurmountable challenge. I stuck to my plan.

I can remember going up to the cottage for Thanksgiving weekend during my first term at McGill. It was the first time in five weeks I'd taken a break from my studies. I hadn't seen my brothers and sisters since starting law school, and the fall colours were at their glorious peak. I'd brought along a mountain of work and spent every spare moment reading my law books. Occasionally I noticed Mom and Dad watching me, but kept going. Halfway through the second day they called me over and sat me down at the kitchen table, just the two of them and me, alone. They both looked at me and said, "Tom, you look tired." I said I was, the work was hard, I was the youngest in my class, and the amount of reading I had to do was just phenomenal. Then they said something I'll never forget as long as I live. "We just want you to know we'll still love you if things don't work out and you decide not to continue law school." Suddenly a great weight was lifted from my shoulders. It was such a relief to hear them say it. The pressure was off, and from then on I worked just as hard but it felt much easier. With regard to my learning French, however, Dad kept after me. Having two languages was a tremendous asset, he said, and I promised him that once I'd completed my law studies I would become fluently bilingual. I kept my promise, largely thanks to my wife, Catherine.

While it had been commonplace in the late fifties and early sixties for families with a mixed linguistic background, like ours, to send their kids to English school, things really began to change after the Quiet Revolution. In fact, the language of education was to become a major political flashpoint and feed the province's most heated linguistic debates for decades to come. Québecers cannot afford to forget that right up until the early sixties, some department stores in downtown Montréal wouldn't even serve their customers in French, the language most of them spoke. Many professional or commercial services were not offered in French. Under successive governments, different formulas were applied to try to ensure that services were available in French and that immigrants to the province learned the majority language. That evolution in Québec society found an echo in our home.

Toward the end of the sixties, Mom resolved to see to it that we kids had a stronger grounding in French. Immersion classes were yet to come fully on stream, so the only real course of action was to send our younger brothers and sisters to French school. Mom's own little Quiet Revolution had Dad's full backing. I can remember Colleen and I holding our own family council on this big change in our lives. How were we going to be able to help the younger kids with their homework? Heck, what if they wouldn't speak English with us anymore? The good news is that we were allowed, as was often the case, to have a full discussion with our parents and get adult answers to our questions. Mom explained that she wanted to make sure that her heritage, her part of who we were, was equally present in our lives. Dad backed Mom all the way and made it clear that, since we were living in Québec, French was going to become far more prevalent in our everyday life, and learning it would be to our advantage in the future.

And so it was. For several more years, while we were still in Laval, and later after the family moved to the Laurentians, most of our younger brothers and sisters received the bulk of their primary education in French, but went on to English secondary school. By chance, most of them wound up founding their families and making their lives in other provinces. Of the four of us who still live in Québec — Jeannie, Danny, Sean, and me — only the youngest, Sean, was educated in French elementary school. Needless to say, we all speak French to this day.

The fact that I was raised in both cultures and languages has always made it easier for me to understand other people's points of view, especially on the matters of culture and language that are so much a part of the Canadian identity and so fundamental to who we are as Canadians. Throughout my career, I've wound up playing a role in language issues that have cropped up in Québec and elsewhere in Canada. During my stints at Justice and at the *Conseil de la langue française* in Québec City, at Alliance Québec in Montréal, or supervising the translation of the Manitoba statutes, or at the *Commission d'appel sur la langue d'enseignement*, I've tried to apply the values I learned at home — values of fairness, respect for others, and the commitment to protect and maintain minority language rights. These are the values that we as Canadians share.

After becoming a member of Parliament, I presented a Bill that would have patched a hole in existing linguistic guarantees. Right now, in Québec, French-speaking employees have a right to receive written instructions from their employer in their own language. The rule applies to anyone who comes under the Québec provincial Labour Code. However, for French-speaking workers of the federally regulated sector, no such right exists. So a person whose first language is French and who works in a bank, a telecommunications company or, for that matter, the Gatineau public transit service (which is federally regulated because the buses cross over into Ontario) has to rely on the goodwill of the employer. When I first tabled the legislation, Michel Sparer, who'd been my colleague at the *Conseil de la langue française* back in the day, wrote an eloquent op-ed in *Le Devoir* on this subject. Curiously, the federal Liberals came out strongly against the proposal as did, more predictably, the Conservatives.

After the Orange Wave brought him to Parliament, Robert Aubin, our Québec caucus chair and MP for Trois-Rivières, took up the cudgel and reintroduced the Bill, but we haven't yet been able to convince the other parties in Parliament to leave partisanship aside and vote for a measure that can only strengthen us as a country. One of our colleagues who worked successfully on a similar measure was Québec City MP Alexandrine Latendresse, who presented a Bill requiring prominent officers of Parliament, such as the Auditor General, to have a working knowledge of both official languages. Thanks to Alexandrine's courage, determination, and hard work, that Bill was adopted unanimously and is now part of Canadian law.

Chapter Two
Learning the Law

As I was heading to university, big changes were underway for my family. Dad had completed his last full year with Armstrong and Taylor in 1973. By the time I started law school in September, he had sold the house in Chomedey and moved the eight younger kids (by then my sister Colleen was already working as a nurse) up north to the cottage, which had been winterized and upgraded with a foundation. I had worked during the summer and had enough money for my tuition, but when I applied for my bursaries and loans, the government factored in my father's income tax returns from 1972 when he'd had a good job. My application was turned down. I was very nearly forced to quit university. For weeks while we all tried to figure out what I could do, I slept on the couch in the small office that Dad sublet with an insurance broker colleague on Monkland Avenue in N.D.G. In the meantime I went to my classes. Since I couldn't afford books, Colleen lent me the money to buy the ones I needed most.

In the end, somehow, and to this day I still don't know how they did it, my parents figured out a way to keep the promise they'd made to me when they couldn't pay for me to go to Loyola High School. During the time I was living on the couch in the Monkland Avenue office, they gave me a series of postdated cheques for $125 each month to tide me over till my student loans could be sorted out. I found a room on Aylmer Street in the McGill student ghetto for $64 a month. I'd have $15 a week for expenses, and that's what I lived on. Luckily for me, McGill as an institution was well endowed and I was able to get a couple of bursaries, the first of which bore the name Mary M. Beattie. I never knew her, but that person's generosity, many years earlier, made it possible for me to get through my first year of law school. When I finished university I had student loans to pay back. But, to give some perspective, after graduating with two degrees from one of the world's top universities I owed a total of about $7,000. Young people today have no such luck. By the time they finish university, many of them owe the equivalent of one-and-a-half to two years' starting salary in their chosen field. It's grossly unfair. It also discourages too many who want to pursue post-secondary studies from ever going to university. It's tragic for them, and a huge loss to society and to this country as a whole. No one who has the marks and the will to further their education should ever be hindered from doing so because of high tuition and the prospect of a terrifying debt load for years and years afterward.

Being so young, I was on a very steep learning curve. I studied in the McLennan Library and was always the last to leave when it closed at midnight. The amount of reading we had to do was phenomenal, and since at that early stage I couldn't know what was important and what wasn't, I read everything. The pace was gruelling. On the first day of lectures the professor warned, "Look to your right, and now look to your left. One of you will no longer be here at Christmas."

Thankfully, some of the teachers were very kind and approachable. In first year every student had a tutor with whom we met once a week to discuss our assigned readings. It was a smart way of keeping us grounded and following our progress. My tutor was a young professor just back from the United States, where he'd earned a Ph.D. in law. We got along very well. Many years later he would go on to be Canada's justice minister. Even though we always sat on different sides of the House, I could never see him as an adversary. His name is Irwin Cotler, and we've remained friends.

One of the most memorable experiences of my first year of law school was meeting Frank R. Scott, the renowned constitutional scholar, champion of civil rights, emeritus law professor, and poet, who gave us a special lecture series that fall. Professor Scott was a legendary figure in the McGill community, having been a founding member of the CCF (the Co-operative Commonwealth Federation), which later evolved into the NDP. He had taken the Québec provincial government to court over its draconian "Padlock Law," a particularly egregious piece of legislation that was officially called the Act to Protect the Province Against Communistic Propaganda and had been introduced in 1937 at the behest of the premier, Maurice Duplessis, who'd named himself attorney general. It severely restricted freedom of speech and denied the presumption of innocence to anyone suspected of communist (but curiously enough, not fascist) leanings. It was so broad, so sweeping and ill defined that it could be used, and often was, against unionized workers protesting the low pay and appalling conditions in the sweatshops of the garment trade in Montréal's industrial East End. One of the most important cases that Frank R. Scott ever took on as a lawyer was *Roncarelli v. Duplessis*, which he successfully fought all the way to the Supreme Court. Frank Roncarelli was a restaurant owner who had had the audacity to help pay the defence of Jehovah's Witnesses who were being persecuted by Duplessis under his Padlock Law. For his efforts, Roncarelli had his liquor licence removed by Duplessis himself in his role as attorney general. Duplessis's downfall in that epic judgment remains a highlight in the annals of Canadian human rights law. Learning what laws can do, for good or ill, to transform society was a revelation. We hadn't yet given ourselves a Charter of Rights and Freedoms, so Professor Scott's lectures were a real eye-opener in terms of right and wrong as applied to public policy.

The moral perspective that Professor Scott brought to discussing the law is even more relevant today. Indeed, the excessively broad, all-encompassing nature of the Harper government's new anti-terror legislation — Bill C-51 — carries disturbing echoes of Duplessis's Padlock Law, right down to the way it was announced at a campaign-style event by Stephen Harper himself, far from Parliament, and using words that conflate terrorism with Islam. In the present context, where Islamophobia seems well on its way to becoming as mainstream and uncontroversial a form of discrimination as it is in the most right-wing corners of Europe, F.R. Scott's legacy and example are more timely than ever.

As revered as he was, Professor Scott was incredibly modest, with the utter lack of pretension that is found only in truly great individuals. He was also extremely generous, kind, engaging, and open-minded, often leavening his lectures with gentle humour. I remember him recounting how he'd been given such a good reception at the Supreme Court that he'd been allowed to move into the forward area reserved at the time for senior lawyers who were QCs (Queen's Counsels), and joking that this meant that he'd been "QC-fied" in the Supreme Court.

Even though McGill was world renowned as an institution of higher learning, like many other schools it was undergoing profound social changes. Manon Vennat, a friend and highly successful lawyer, told me that in 1965 when she was at McGill, she had been one of only three women in her law class. By the time I got there, eight years later, women still represented only about a third of the students in the faculty. The year was 1973, which doesn't seem so long ago, yet that year's annual *Martin's Criminal Code* still listed flogging with a cat-o'-nine-tails as one of the punishments judges could impose in a whole variety of cases. And let's not forget that Canada was still running the infamous Indian residential schools program, an atrocity that robbed generations of First Nations children of their parents, their childhood, and their identity, leaving many of them traumatized for life because of the abuse they endured. But the times, as Bob Dylan sang, were a-changin'. McGill had always been an exclusive Anglo-Saxon institution in a province and city where the majority were French speaking. Four years before my first year at McGill, on March 28, 1969, 10,000 students had marched on the university, staging a massive protest known as *McGill français*. The protest was the result of an alliance between nationalist students from other Québec universities and young progressives at McGill. Among them was a young McGill student named Jack Layton.

Elsewhere in Québec great changes were afoot on many policy fronts. Within a few weeks of my starting law school, Québec Superior Court Justice Albert Malouf handed down a landmark decision granting the Crees and Inuit of Northern Québec an injunction to block construction of the Québec government's massive James Bay hydroelectric dam until the province had negotiated an agreement with the indigenous peoples of the area. At the time this was the largest engineering project in Canada. Premier Bourassa moved quickly, delegating as his personal representative John Ciaccia, who in 1994 became my officemate in Opposition when I was first elected as a member of the *Assemblée nationale*. Ciaccia sat down with the Cree and Inuit representatives and the two parties began negotiations. The result two years later was the landmark James Bay and Northern Quebec Agreement, which acquired constitutional status in 1982 when Canada's Constitution was patriated from London. It has since become a model for modern treaty making in Canada. It began a process that led to establishing a genuine nation-to-nation relationship between the Québec government and First Nations, as well as the Inuit of Nunavik. Today there is actually a Cree embassy in Québec City.

My first year in law school was also the year I joined the NDP. A classmate of mine named Gabor Zinner, who was very smart and a real character, wanted to be a candidate in the upcoming federal election. The NDP was known as the party of Tommy Douglas, the man who in 1961, as premier of Saskatchewan, had introduced medicare in his province, the first publicly funded health-care plan of its kind in Canada. Tommy Douglas was also the man who in 1970, as federal NDP leader, had stood on principle and denounced the imposition of the War Measures Act. I had come close to meeting Tommy Douglas myself in the summer of 1965, when I was ten. My grade six teacher, Ron Beauvais, who drove a beat-up old Pontiac with an NDP bumper-sticker on the back fender, recently told me that he was responsible for an event that I remember to this day. One day that summer I spotted a commotion on the other side of the park across the street from where we lived. There were people honking their horns, hooting and hollering and holding signs, and making a little parade for someone who was riding along in an open convertible. I asked my father, "Who's that?"

"That's Tommy Douglas."

"Who's he?"

"He's the head of the NDP."

"Is that like the Liberals or the Conservatives?"

"No, no, no, it's another party."

"What does that party do?"

"They stand up for the little guy, like me," answered Dad, which struck me as funny at the time, because he was an imposing six feet tall and weighed 240 pounds.

"So are you going to vote for him?"

"Oh no, they don't have a chance in Québec."

It's just an anecdote, but it's reflective of the time, because back then in Québec, if you had a social conscience or social democratic leanings, you didn't have a voice. That was the dynamic until the Orange Wave led by Jack Layton swept the province in 2011.

My friend Gabor, along with a bunch of us who supported him and had obtained our NDP memberships, piled into a car and headed for Vanier College, where the nomination meeting was being held. The guy who gave the opening speech at the beginning of the meeting was the president of the NDP's Québec wing. He had run unsuccessfully for the party the previous year in the riding of Outremont. His name was Henri-François Gautrin, and eventually he went on to become the Liberal MNA for Verdun and a dear colleague of mine in the *Assemblée nationale* and in Cabinet.

Chapter Three
Catherine

In the summer of 1974 I was nineteen years old and I had just completed my first year at law school. A dear friend's sister got married that summer. The families gathered on a beautiful July day in the Laurentians. At the reception after the ceremony my best friend Wayne Hellstrom and I were put in charge of the bar by the lake. At one point there appeared a girl I had never seen before. She was very striking, very beautiful, with a sensitive, thoughtful face, eyes that shone brightly, and a radiant smile. Her name was Catherine Pinhas, and she was a cousin of the groom. She told me that she'd just arrived from Paris and was representing the French side of the family. I loved the way she spoke, the music of her French. She was a real beauty who stood out amongst all the guests.

That evening a group of the younger attendees wound up hanging out together. There were other cousins in, too, from France and Sweden. We all concocted a plan to go to Old Montréal together. I had spent much of the evening speaking with Catherine and looked forward to the outing. Our trip to Old Montréal with Catherine, her cousins, and other friends (we were seven in a Mazda) turned out to be Catherine's and my first date. It was a road show. We spent all of our free time together for the next few weeks, and Catherine pushed back the date of her return to France. I soon introduced her to my family. Our life was so different from anything she'd experienced. She'd grown up with one sister in a very straitlaced, tony neighbourhood of Paris. My family was rough-and-tumble, with children all over the place and people who made four sandwiches out of one chicken wing, and who said "I love you" all day. Dad was a big, imposing man who often shouted to be heard in our noisy household. To Catherine at first he seemed a bear, until she realized he was really just a lovable teddy bear. Catherine and my mom hit it off right away. Catherine has always said that my mom is a saint.

As I took her around the Laurentians, the beauty of the landscape, the wide-open spaces, and even my family enchanted her. We became inseparable. By the end of her stay we had fallen deeply in love. To me, being a logical, practical kind of guy, her returning a continent away left a huge question mark. Pursuing a relationship with her across five thousand kilometres of ocean just seemed so difficult. But Catherine, who believes that with a little effort, will, and imagination you can overcome any obstacle, reassured me. She would simply announce to her parents that she'd met the man she was going to marry and that she was going right back to him.

Of course, when she got there and informed them of her plans — showing them a picture of me with hair halfway down to my elbows and a beard, dressed in white overalls and a white Indian tunic — they were appalled. After all, aside from the fact she was just nineteen and they didn't know me from Adam, the original purpose of sending their daughter to that wedding had been to stop her from going off to Greece to celebrate passing her French *baccalauréat* with friends they disapproved of. Add to that the fact that we were from totally different backgrounds, and her parents had good reason to feel worried. Their family was well to do and lived in Neuilly, a wealthy, upper-middle-class suburb of Paris. Culturally, too, we couldn't have been more different. I was from a devout Catholic family, while her parents were Sephardic Jews, originally from Turkey, who had been very young during the German Occupation and had survived the Holocaust, while many of their relatives had not. Catherine and her sister Brigitte were kept in the dark about that part of their parents' lives while they were growing up. It was never mentioned, a place of immense pain that they never spoke of and didn't want their daughters to ever have to know about.

Catherine and Brigitte had had very little religious upbringing beyond tradition. That, I was to learn, was all too common with people who had suffered that indescribable fear and trauma. Her parents, just like the father of her Canadian cousin, seemed far more open to talking with me about it. The stories came out slowly. Stories of courage. Of survival: how Catherine's mom, Lydia, had escaped in the night with her parents, just before her eleventh birthday, to what was then still the unoccupied part of France. In a town called Aurillac she would spend three years with her parents, living in an attic. How her dad, Raphaël, had seen his father, Nissim, and then his sister, Ida, taken by the French to the Drancy internment camp for deportation. Another part of the history is that Generalissimo Franco was issuing Spanish passports to Sephardic Jews, the descendants of Jews who had been expelled from Spain by Queen Isabella four hundred and fifty years earlier, in 1492. Thanks to that gesture, that part of Catherine's family went to Spain and were able to survive the war. In the summer of 2014, Catherine and I took Lydia back to Aurillac for the first time since the war. She was able to show us around with the eyes of the young girl that she had been during those years. We even went to the house where she had lived.

Catherine's parents were quite understandably alarmed that their otherwise reasonable daughter had somehow decided, over a summer holiday in Canada, that she was going to spend the rest of her life with the guy in that picture. When Catherine couldn't be dissuaded from carrying out our crazy plan, her parents convinced her to at least wait until Christmas, so that I could come to Paris to meet them. At the end of the fall term I cut my hair to shoulder length, trimmed my beard, and flew to Paris. Arriving from the airport with Catherine, I remember walking through the entranceway to the magnificent building where her family lived and feeling slightly intimidated. By pure chance we bumped into her parents in the courtyard, and it was a bit of luck that allowed us to break the ice. Her mom, still in her early forties, was the incarnation of Paris chic. Her dad, who I was soon to learn had a delightful sense of humour, cracked a joke or two, clearly intending to put me at ease. It worked. They went off to do an errand while Catherine and I breathed a sigh of relief that it had gone so well. The trip allowed us both to realize that this was real.

We'd written to each other every single day, and after my return to Canada we continued doing so. We still have the hundreds of letters that we each wrote over the two-year period from our meeting in 1974 to our wedding two years later. The following summer, in 1975, Catherine came to Canada and lived with my brother Peter and me in the apartment the two of us shared in N.D.G. There might have been a slightly different version told to her parents about Catherine staying at the apartment of my sisters Colleen and Jeannie in Westmount, but I'm not sure anyone was fooling anyone else.

That time together was magical. I would bike to work in the morning to Atwater Roofing in Ville Saint-Pierre, the same company where I'd worked for several summers. Exceptions were the days when it was raining. You cannot work with hot tar on those days. So Catherine and I were probably the only two people in Montréal who were thrilled if it was raining in the morning, because it meant we'd be together for the day.

This was to be a short summer in terms of work, however, as Catherine and I had decided we were going to get married. We were both twenty. We informed my parents of our plan and had their blessing — they were both in love with Catherine. She then returned to France a bit before me and gave her own parents enough of a hint so that it was now up to me to formally ask her dad for her hand in marriage. Here the reactions of both our dads are worth retelling.

After Catherine and I spoke to my parents, my dad pulled me aside, and in one of those serious moments where you know you'd better listen, he simply said, "I'm thrilled for both of you, but you'd better understand that this is not like having a girlfriend, then moving on." He was speaking from the heart, and his heart had a serious place for Catherine, and he was making sure that I understood how important this was.

Catherine's dad, predictably, played it both ways. When I asked for Catherine's hand he agreed with tears in his eyes to let me marry his daughter. Then, when we returned to the living room where Catherine and her mom were waiting, he couldn't resist; he told Lydia that he'd given me permission to have their daughter's hand in marriage, but added — laughing — "But I also told him 'no returns.'" That was Rapha. Our parents spoke to each other over the phone and, even though they had never met, they were all thrilled.

Catherine, her parents, and I went for a two-week holiday together in the south of France, and had a tremendous time together. Not only did we all get to know each other more fully, we were also able to finalize plans for the coming year. Since it would be impossible for my family to travel to France, and not all the family in France would be able to come to Canada, we decided that we would have a large engagement party in France at Christmas and get married in Canada the following summer. Catherine came back to Canada with me, because her university term would be late in starting because of a strike. We put a small down payment on an engagement ring that we both really liked and got to spend several more weeks together as I began my final year of my first law degree at McGill.

That ring also has a bit of a story to it. Throughout the fall, whenever I could spare ten or twenty dollars, I'd go to the jewellers and put the cash toward purchasing it. By Christmas it was ours, and I headed off with the lovely ring to see Catherine and her parents in Paris. Catherine's parents picked me up at the airport, and Catherine was in the front seat with her dad on the way home. She turned toward me with that beaming smile and asked me if I had the ring, so she could show her parents. It was my turn to play a practical joke. I produced the Van Woods ring case, in which I'd placed a plastic toy ring that I'd literally found inside a box of Cracker Jack (we still have it). What happened next taught me so much about Catherine.

Instead of looking dismayed or bewildered, she just smiled even more and put it on. When I produced the real one from my pocket we all had a good laugh. Later, when we were alone, I told her how surprised I was that she hadn't reacted more to my prank. Here is where I learned that Catherine is always, first and foremost, concerned for the other person. "Oh, no, *chéri*. You see, I was just afraid that you hadn't been able to buy the other one, and I didn't want to show surprise and hurt your feelings. If it *had* been that ring, it wouldn't have made any difference for me."

We had a beautiful engagement supper with some twenty family members in Neuilly, and then a splendid party in the Bois de Boulogne for a hundred family and friends who would not be able to make it to the wedding in Canada. At one point Catherine and I were going through some papers in preparation for our return to Canada, and I asked her to give me her passport number so that I could jot it down. She said, "Twenty-four ten fifty-four." "No, no, your passport number," I repeated, thinking she had misunderstood. She showed me her passport, and there it was, her passport number, which was also my birthdate. Obviously I had won big in the lottery of life.

I completed my law degree and I was so proud when my parents were able to attend the graduation. Dad broke his "never wear a tie" rule. That summer I had some work in Montréal in construction, but I soon headed to Paris to be with Catherine and her family. While I was there I found work at a heavy equipment manufacturer in Pontoise. I loved it, even though 1976 was one of the hottest summers on record and the factory was stifling. I'd leave very early in the morning in an old Austin Mini, stop for a coffee and a Gauloise (of course) along the way, put in my day's work, and be home for activities with Catherine and her family in the evening. We all set off for Montréal about a week before the wedding, and they met my family for the first time at Mirabel Airport. Catherine's parents, her sister Brigitte, and her grandmother fell in love with my parents: it was family love at first sight. My parents had fixed up an older cottage on the property to accommodate Catherine's family, and we spent a fabulous time together. Catherine loves to tell the story of an exchange between her dad and my mom that speaks volumes about the differences between our two families. My little brother Sean, then five, was wearing one red sock and one green one, and Rapha pointed this out to Jeanne. When you've had ten kids, just making sure they have something on is mission accomplished. "Oh yeah," Mom said, "he probably has another pair just like it in his drawer." Rapha laughed out loud and learned to love that simple informality.

Our wedding was held in the Sainte-Anne-des-Lacs church on July 31, 1976. It was the same church where my parents had been married, and where our son Matthew married Jasmyne some thirty years later. The weather wasn't bad but there was a bit of rain, so we always tell young couples who are getting married not to worry if it rains, because it brings good luck.

The reception was held on my parents' property at Lac Marois. Catherine's grandmother had not been thrilled at the idea of her getting married in a church. Luckily, the monk who married us, a Trappist monk from Oka who had been taking care of the church while the priest was away, said that we didn't have to have a Mass. So inside the church we held what was essentially a civil ceremony that Catherine's grandmother was able to attend, and everybody was happy. Afterward, Catherine and I took off on our honeymoon and travelled down to New York. At least we planned to, until we got to the U.S. border. Despite the fact that Catherine was now married to a Canadian citizen, she didn't yet have a Canadian passport, and when she showed her French passport they wouldn't let her in. This presented a huge problem because we'd agreed to meet up with her parents and grandmother (who had taken the trouble to get visas in France, whereas I'd incorrectly presumed that since Catherine and I were married, she would be able to travel on my passport) days later, at the top of the Empire State Building. By then they'd already left. Of course this was all long before cell-phones, so we had no way to get in touch with them to let them know what had happened. Luckily, the border guard that day was the world's nicest person. After much pleading he let us in on the strength of my passport alone, and we continued on our journey.

We took a romantic four days together, meandering through the mountains of upstate New York, after which we joined Catherine's parents in New York City. I often joke that I spent my honeymoon with my in-laws, but we all had a fabulous time. It did give rise to a famous family anecdote, when at one point Catherine's parents and grandmother decided to go shopping and were almost two hours late returning. When they finally showed up and I asked what had happened, Catherine's dad, who was still laughing, suggested we go and have a cup of coffee so he could explain. *Mamie,* as Catherine called her grandmother, said she had some American money that had made it through the war. Her husband had brought it back after working several years in the United States around the time of the First World War. Much later, after the Second World War had broken out and they'd had to go into hiding, *Mamie* had rolled the bills down to the size of cigarettes and sewn them into the seams of her undergarment. When the time came to pay for her purchases and she pulled out these tight little rolls of hundred-dollar bills from the early 1900s, unrolling them on the sales counter at Bloomingdale's, the sales clerk called security. *Mamie,* Rapha, and Lydia were escorted "upstairs" to the security office, where the person in charge, after examining the bills, declared them perfectly legal tender, so in the end the store accepted the payment. Needless to say, those bills belonged in someone's collection, not in a cash register. We then went to Niagara Falls and to Ottawa before heading back to Montréal. One of the pictures I have from that trip, taken by Catherine, is of me standing in front of the Parliament Buildings.

Catherine and I got an apartment on Sherbrooke Street in Montréal, in the same building where I'd lived with my brother Peter. We had barely any furniture and had to hang blankets on the windows instead of curtains, but she didn't care. She took a job as a substitute teacher in a primary school in Westmount, insisting that I continue law school and get my second law degree rather than quit and get a full-time job. She knew that that was what I wanted to do and she feared that if I quit I wouldn't get the chance to go back.

That first winter Catherine didn't know how to walk in the snow, and she kept slipping and falling down. Once when she got off the bus at McTavish and Sherbrooke, on her way to come pick me up at the law faculty, she slipped and swan-dived into the snow as a passerby tried to catch her. When he asked her if she was "still in one piece," an expression she was not familiar with, she laughed so hard that she couldn't get back on her feet again. At her school, when her turn came to supervise the kids at recess, they would huddle around her and help her to shuffle very slowly to the middle of the schoolyard. When the recess ended, they'd gather around and shepherd her back to the door of the school. Those kids adored her, and she loved them.

Perhaps because of what her family had gone through, Catherine has always been extremely open to and respectful of others. She is one of the few people I know who always, always, softly but firmly, speaks up and intervenes whenever she hears anyone make an intolerant remark or joke about someone else's religion or background. Catherine has a crystal-clear sense of priorities. Her core values of respect for all human beings, of love of family and friends, of honesty and loyalty, have always inspired me and our sons.

Catherine became a true Canadian hockey mom through the years I coached our son Greg's team. Once, when we were all watching the world juniors, which were being held that year in Boston, Catherine pulled me aside and asked, "How far is Boston?" "Five or six hours," I said. Catherine peeked in on the boys. "Would you like to go to Boston and see the final?" They leaped. So a Catherine-inspired, totally spontaneous family trip ensued. We had no trouble getting tickets, because even the final was sparsely attended. We overnighted in Boston and had a ball. That's Catherine. Creating an unforgettable family moment that we all talk about to this day. She is also the doting mom, who can sometimes gently prod her kids to push themselves.

When Matt finished high school, he was admitted to the three-year police technologies course at John Abbott College. You need really good marks to get in, and Matt was a top student. Catherine also felt that he could, and should, continue to study. When Matt was a young police officer with a full-time job, still living at home, Catherine made him an offer he couldn't refuse: "Continue your studies part-time, we'll pay the books and tuition, and as long as you do study, you won't have to pay room and board at home." While Matt continued his studies in administration at McGill, Greg began his at the Faculty of Engineering. We were so happy and proud when both of them graduated in the same week in 2005. Matt's studies at McGill have helped him in his career, and he is now a sergeant in the *Sûreté du Québec* (Québec Provincial Police). Greg went on to do a master's degree in aerospace engineering at École Polytechnique and is a full-time professor of physics and engineering technology at John Abbott.

All families, even the happiest, go through moments of pain and sorrow. Ours is no different. One tragic event that happened to us has had a lasting effect on Catherine and her family in France, as well as ours in Canada. On a Saturday morning in early 1996, Catherine woke up suddenly and simply said, "There's something wrong, I have to phone my parents." She was fully awake in an instant, and when I asked what she meant, she just answered, "I don't know what, but there's something terribly wrong."

She went downstairs and immediately called them. I was beside her and recall that her very first words, when her mom answered, were not "Hello, how are you?" but rather, "What's happened? What's going on?"

Her mom explained that because of the time difference they'd been waiting to call. The day before, Catherine's little sister Brigitte, after weeks of severe headaches, had been sent for an X-ray. The news was devastating. She had a brain tumour of a kind that was particularly aggressive. Catherine packed and took the next plane to be in Paris with Brigitte and her family. At the time, Brigitte and Jean-Luc's two children, Emma and Martin, were four and one. Jean-Luc was devastated, as we all were, but he remained a pillar of strength. Through several operations and treatments, Brigitte miraculously came to be well enough to travel with Jean-Luc and the kids to be with us in the Laurentians for an unforgettable time that summer. Catherine travelled frequently back and forth to Paris, to be with her parents and to support Brigitte and her family, even if it was only for a couple of days at a time.

In May 1997 Brigitte left us, after a courageous battle. Friends and family gathered in the imposing cemetery where she was laid to rest. We were all inconsolable. Emma and Martin were heartbroken, and my brother-in-law, Jean-Luc, had lost the love of his life. Catherine and her parents were resolute in their determination to continue to help them as much as possible.

A section of the Outremont war memorial, with my uncle's name, "T.C. Mulcair," among those of the fallen.

An early photo of my mom, Jeanne Hurtubise, and my dad, Harry Mulcair.

My high-school basketball team. I am in the front row, fifth from the left.

Waiting to depart on a school trip to Europe with my classmates, age fourteen. I am in the back row, sixth from the right.

With my mom and dad, the day of my high school graduation.

With my brother Peter (left).

The Mulcair family cottage at Lac Marois, Québec.

My siblings and I (second from left) gather to celebrate our parents' twenty-fifth wedding anniversary in Saint-Sauveur, Québec, on July 26, 1977.

Father Cox teaching at Laval Catholic High School.

Father Cox with Mother Teresa during her visit to Laval Catholic High School in 1988.

In my Québec City office as president of the Office des professions du Québec, *a position I held from 1987 to 1993.*

Presenting a reform package to Québec's professional governing boards in 1991.

With the members of the Office des professions du Québec.

With my sons, Greg, age five, and Matt, age nine, at home in Beaconsfield, Québec.

My six sisters and Catherine. From left to right: Colleen, Sheilagh, Deb, Maureen (in front), Catherine, Kelly, and Jeannie.

A family gathering in Nice, France, in 1990. From left to right: Catherine; our son Greg; brother-in-law Jean-Luc Glock; our eldest son, Matt; and on the right, next to me, Catherine's mom, Lydia; Catherine's sister, Brigitte; and their dad, Raphaël.

Matt and Greg in Austria in 1990.

With Matt in Ireland (1991).

Coaching Greg's hockey team in 1991. Greg is in the front row, second from right.

With my brothers and Graham Carpenter, who would later become my riding office manager in Chomedey and Outremont, at my youngest brother Sean's wedding. From left to right: Sean, Danny, me, Peter, and Graham, the best man.

Rooting for Canada at the 1996 World Junior Ice Hockey Championships in Boston with Matt and Greg. Canada won!

Catherine's family. In the back, from left to right: her mom, Lydia; her dad, Raphaël; her niece, Emma; and her brother-in-law, Jean-Luc Glock. In the front: her sister, Brigitte; and her nephew, Martin.

With my sisters Deb and Sheilagh on the day that Deb received her Ph.D. from the University of Calgary.

With volunteer Jeanine Papineau in front of the former family home on the corner of 99th Avenue and 2nd Street in Laval, on the first day of my first election campaign in the provincial riding of Chomedey, in 1994.

Campaigning at the Henri-Bourassa Metro and Bus Terminal in Montréal during the 1994 Québec election.

With Daniel Johnson and his wife, Suzanne Marcil, campaigning for the "No" side during the 1995 Québec Referendum.

With René Dussault, who co-chaired the 1996 Royal Commission on Aboriginal Peoples, at a dinner marking the twenty-fifth anniversary of the Office des professions du Québec. Left to right: Jean K. Samson, former deputy minister of justice and then president of the Office des professions du Québec; founding president René Dussault; Linda Goupil, PQ minister in charge of the professions; Ginette Pepin, the secretary to me and all the other presidents; and Robert Diamant, my successor at Office des professions du Québec.

Saturday, February 28th, 1998/Samedi le 28 février 1998
Arène Lakeshore Arena 12:30 P.M./12h30

SATURDAY GAME LINE-UP

ASSEMBLÉE NATIONALE DU QUÉBEC	LEGISLATIVE ASSEMBLY OF ONTARIO
1 Claude BEAULIEU	1 Gary CARR, Oakville South
1 Rick MOFFATT, CJAD	2 Marcel BEAUBIEN, Lambton
2 Tom KENNEDY, CBC	3 Jim BROWN, Scarborough West
3 Gilles MORIN, Radio-Canada	4 John OAKLEY, CFRB
4 Norman MacMILLAN, Papineau	6 Hon. Dave JOHNSON, Don Mills
5 Jocelyn RANCOURT	7 Bill GRIMMETT, Muskoka-Georgian Bay
6 François GENDRON, Abitibi-Ouest	8 Bruce SMITH, Middlesex
7 Jean-Guy PARÉ, Lotbinière	9 Hon. Mike HARRIS, Nipissing, Premier
8 Geoffrey KELLY, Jacques-Cartier	10 Hon. Jim FLAHERTY, Durham Centre
9 Georges FARRAH, Îles-de-la-Madeleine	11 Jerry OUELLETTE, Oshawa
10 Michel LÉTOURNEAU, Ungava	13 Gary STEWART, Peterborough
11 Rhéal SÉGUIN, Globe and Mail	14 John O'TOOLE, Durham East
13 Claude BOUCHER, Johnson	16 Frank KLEES, York-MacKenzie
14 Christian BARRETTE	18 Morley KELLS, Etobicoke-Lakeshore
15 Marcel LANDRY, Bonaventure	19 John PARKER, York East
16 Thomas MULCAIR, Chomedey	20 Ron JOHNSON, Brantford
17 Benoît SAVARD	22 Hon. Chris STOCKWELL, Etobicoke West,
18 Jean SÉGUIN	Speaker
18 Rob KEMP, CJAD	26 Bart MAVES, Niagara Falls
19 René LECAVALIER	27 Hon. Bob RUNCIMAN, Leeds-Grenville
21 François LAROCHELLE, CTV	30 Paul MOTT, CFRB
	44 Tom FROESE, St. Catharines - Brock

Entraôneur / Coach
Hon. Jean- Pierre CHARBONNEAU,
Borduas, Président / Speaker
Entraôneur / Coach
Russell WILLIAMS, Nelligan

Coach / Entraôneur
Gary FOX, Prince Edward-Lennox
Coach / Entraôneur
Gary LEADSTON, Kitchener-Wilmot
Coach / Entraôneur
Bob McALLISTER

The line-up for the Assemblée nationale *vs. Legislative Assembly of Ontario hockey game in 1998.*

The players of the friendly match between the Québec and Ontario legislatures. I am in the middle row, third from the left. Jim Flaherty is in the front row, fourth from the right.

Chapter Four
Making Ends Meet

For the first couple of years after getting married we continued to live in our small apartment. We didn't have much, but it didn't matter. We got hold of some orange crates and used them as shelving, as stands for knick-knacks, and as bedside tables. One day, one of Catherine's uncles came to visit; when he saw the crates he said we'd furnished our apartment in *Louis Caisse*, a play on words in reference to the French *Louis Quinze* (King Louis XV) style of furniture. We still have those crates and we treasure them. We've always kept them around our home, as symbols and as reminders of what's important.

Before we were married, while I was in third year at McGill, I had run for president of the Law Students' Association, then called the Law Undergraduate Society, or LUS. This time I had better luck than in high school. In the fall of 1975, as I began the academic year, Catherine was still in Montréal owing to the strike at her university in France. As the new LUS president, I had to deliver a speech to incoming students. Since the speech was to be in English and French, Catherine wrote every word of the French. She remains my closest adviser for all my speeches.

I finished my second law degree, a Bachelor of Laws (LL.B.) in common law, in 1977. Our son Matt was born in 1978, when I was reading for the Bar. Right away I was offered a job at the Justice Department in Québec City, because the one expert they had at common law was on maternity leave. Going straight from law school into the Legislative Affairs Branch — the part of the Québec Justice Department where laws are drafted — was an incredible opportunity, a bit like getting sent to an exclusive finishing school and being paid to be there. The people I got to work with at Justice were among the best legal minds in the country. My immediate supervisor was a top professor from Laval University named Denis Carrier, a demanding taskmaster who has remained a lifelong friend. My *maître de stage*, the person who oversaw my clerkship to the Québec Bar, was Gilles Létourneau, who had a Ph.D. in law from the London School of Economics and who went on to become a very distinguished judge of the Federal Court. I was thrilled when he called me, after I became leader of the NDP, to go out to supper. Even though we reminisced about old times, we also discussed military law, one of his areas of expertise, at great length. Gilles had in fact chaired the Commission of Inquiry into the Deployment of Canadian Forces to Somalia in the 1990s.

The legislative branch is one of the most fascinating areas of government in which to work. It's the place where policy ideas are given legal meaning and shaped into instruments that will then produce results in concrete terms. Another thing I learned is that people in the legislative branch can — and sometimes do — nudge the wording of a law in a direction they happen to favour. This is one of the many reasons why, in the British parliamentary system, draft legislation must go through close and careful scrutiny by members of Parliament or provincial legislatures and then receive a second reading after amendments have been added. Unconscionably, these time-honoured parliamentary procedures designed to ensure that our laws are properly vetted and serve the public interest have been systematically flouted, trampled, and overridden by Mr. Harper's Conservatives in the House of Commons. With their governing majority, within a single electoral mandate, Stephen Harper and his MPs have shut down debate more than one hundred times, thus severely limiting needed debate and preventing close parliamentary scrutiny more frequently than any government in Canadian history.

When I arrived at the legislative branch, the deputy minister of justice was René Dussault, another distinguished law professor, who later became a judge of the Québec Court of Appeal. He went on to co-chair the Royal Commission on Aboriginal Peoples, whose report, published in 1996, could have marked a turning point in Canadian history if its recommendations hadn't been left to gather dust ever since. René had a passion for social justice. I remember running into him at a dinner to mark the twenty-fifth anniversary of the *Office des professions du Québec*, which he had helped found and of which we had both been president. By then I'd gone into politics and was an Opposition member of the *Assemblée nationale*. René pulled me aside. He wanted to talk to me about the Royal Commission Report. Before writing it, he'd spent three years travelling across Canada to countless reserves and First Nations communities in the country. "You have to understand," he said, "this is the most urgent issue anyone who is going to stay in Canadian politics has to internalize: this has to be fixed. If we don't get it right, we're going to be leaving a colossal debt on the backs of future generations and we're never going to be able to afford it. Look at the demographics; they're exponential. This is a massive problem, and everybody's trying to ignore it." René Dussault, for those who know him, is not an emotional person. He's a very measured, very Cartesian thinker, who believes in the primacy of reason. But he was very emotional that day, very passionate, because of all that he'd seen and experienced in the previous three years. That conversation with René Dussault has stayed with me ever since. Repairing Canada's relationship with its indigenous peoples is a very complex, very urgent issue, and it has been a top priority for me and our NDP caucus since we became the Official Opposition.

During my first couple of months at the Québec Justice Department, because our son Matt had just been born, I was loath to move my family from Montréal to Québec City until I knew whether I would be given a longer term contract. Every morning I would leave our apartment near Loyola College in the West End, often picking up Jeanne Leclerc-Houde, a colleague who was to become a lead Crown prosecutor in Montréal, at her home on Lorne Crescent near McGill University at 5:00 a.m., and drive to Québec City for 8:00 a.m. Then at 5:00 p.m., after putting in a full day's work, I would drive us both back to Montréal and spend the evening at home with Catherine and Matt.

Finally in September 1978 I got the contract and we moved to Québec City. The day of the move, we packed up our things and I went to rent a truck. But as I was still only twenty-three years old and the age for renting a truck was twenty-five, the car-rental company wouldn't let me have one. I protested that I was an adult, that I had a child, that I was a lawyer, but my driver's licence said I wasn't twenty-five and that was the end of that. This put me in a terrible bind because we had sublet the apartment and had to vacate it that very day. Fortunately, I phoned our friend Jean-Claude Pilon and told him of my predicament. He came right over, rented the truck, helped me load up our belongings, and drove it to Québec City. There he helped me unload it and then he drove it all the way back to Montréal. Everyone should be lucky enough to have such friends.

For me, the job at Justice was also a great opportunity to perfect my written French. By then my spoken skills had vastly improved thanks to Catherine and all the practice I got hanging out with our young French-speaking friends. As I'd never studied in French, though, my written skills still left much to be desired. At the outset, Catherine would spend countless hours at night helping me with my written French presentations. On that score I also owe Lise Vézeau, the secretary of the office in which I worked at Justice, a huge debt of gratitude. She made a deal with me. She promised to help me with my French, but only on one condition: that when I submitted something in writing, I was to sit beside her and let her point out my mistakes, explaining the rules of French grammar and how to correct my errors myself. "Although they sound the same, endings in *é, er,* and *ez* are not interchangeable," she would remind me with a smile. She, too, was part of the coaching process. By the end of my two-and-a-half-year stint, my written French and grammar had been upgraded considerably.

During my time at Justice I worked a great deal on preparing legislative drafting guides. That's when I first met Michel Sparer, who'd published some groundbreaking work on legislative drafting that was inspired more by French civil law techniques than the long enumeration of jurisprudence found in most common law legislation at the time. I went on to publish a 300-page bibliography on the topic, while Michel and another friend, Wallace Schwab, published a remarkable work outlining their approach and a critique of current drafting methods.

It sounds like such an arcane subject, but if we were going to have a country that was at once bilingual and blessed with two legal systems, we had to make sure that our laws as drafted in one language and legal system were equally intelligible in the other. We had very lively debates with Elmer Driedger, a widely regarded expert who was the leading authority on legislative drafting and statutory interpretation. I'd had occasion to meet with Mr. Driedger, who was a truly gracious man and whose many works on the subject were gospel to the legal profession throughout the Commonwealth. Nevertheless, Driedger was largely insensitive to the central argument put forward by Michel Sparer, which was that much of the legislation contained in our federal statute book was drafted in ways that didn't make a lot of sense from a civil law perspective.

Then, around 1980, Gérard Bertrand, a superb legislative drafter and jurist then working in Ottawa, took up the challenge. As head of the legislative drafting branch in the federal Justice Department and the first French-speaking jurist in that position — he was the main drafter of the Canadian Charter of Rights and Freedoms in 1980–81 — Bertrand established a system of co-drafting. Thanks to his work, today in Canada each of the English and French texts of our statutes are original versions. They are identical, of course, as a matter of law, but they are no longer literal, word-for-word translations. This is why, if you were to put the two versions of a law side by side, you'd find that the various sections aren't necessarily numbered identically, reflecting the different ways in which thoughts and propositions are organized and structured in French and English.

When I was working in the legislative branch at Justice in Québec City, we knew that before a Bill was presented by the government for consideration by the *Assemblée nationale,* all of our work would wind up before the *Comité de législation du Conseil exécutif,* the legislative committee of Cabinet that was the ultimate arbiter of the form and substance of every piece of legislation. Those committee members were an impressive crew and, to a young lawyer just earning his spurs, a bit intimidating. Much later, when as a Cabinet minister I was invited to sit on the *Comité de législation,* I was delighted to find that several friends and colleagues with whom I'd worked some twenty-five years earlier were now the senior counsel to the committee. I was even more thrilled when, in 2005, Premier Charest asked me to become the chair of that body. It was a rewarding position; I'd come full circle on a subject that had opened many doors for me during my career.

When I say that for me, getting a job at the Québec Justice Department was like being sent to an exclusive finishing school, I mean that, having gone to McGill so young, I may have been able to catch up and get through law school, but the Québec Justice Department is where I actually learned the law. I loved my job so much that in 1980 I applied for a permanent position in the civil service, because I wanted to be hired right where I was, at Justice. You had to put in your name to get on the list of candidates, and then to qualify by passing the exams. I finished first, which meant that my name that my name was first on the list for all departments, and I found myself "drafted" by the *Conseil de la langue française,* an advisory body created by the Lévesque government under Bill 101, the Charter of the French Language. Not to be confused with the *Office de la langue française,* which supervised the application and enforcement of Bill 101, the *Conseil* had as its mission to counsel the minister responsible for the application of the Charter of the French language on any question relative to the French language in Québec.

At the time, the political context in Québec was dramatically different from what it is today. By the early 1970s the language issue had reached full boil. The October Crisis had terrified the province. The invocation of the War Measures Act, giving the army and police extraordinary powers that led to the arbitrary arrest and detention without charge of hundreds of innocent people, inflamed the cleavages already dividing the population. The Parti Québécois victory in the election of 1976 had stunned everyone, and as a lawyer in the legislative drafting branch of the Québec Justice Department I had a front row seat on the *projet de société* being presented to Québecers during the first Parti Québécois mandate. In social, economic, and environmental terms, René Lévesque and his government came in on a whirlwind of change, often inspired by the Scandinavian social democratic model. The words *modèle suédois* (Swedish approach) were often a top selling point for any policy proposal. Progressive policies were enacted, among them the Québec Charter of Human Rights and Freedoms (predating the Canadian Charter by six years), a university tuition freeze, public no-fault auto insurance, anti-scab legislation, government regulation of the professions, and the beginnings of publicly subsidized child care.

The *modèle québécois* (Québec approach) that evolved at that time would become emblematic of forward-looking policies that reflect Canadian values of fairness and solidarity. As a progressive, I was truly impressed by the speed and efficiency with which Lévesque and his government were able to effect real change in people's lives. But his was also a government that was preparing to hold a referendum on dismantling Canada. As a Canadian, therefore, I felt a more and more pressing need to get involved and do everything I could to help keep our country together. Up to that point I had never engaged in grassroots political organizing. The biggest campaign I'd ever participated in was my run for president of the Law Undergraduate Society at McGill. I was now a twenty-five-year-old husband and dad, working full-time in government and teaching at Champlain College, and had no idea how to get started. I learned then the truth of the adage attributed to Tip O'Neill, the former Speaker of the U.S. House of Representatives, that "all politics is local."

In Québec, as the referendum approached, sovereignist fervour was at its peak. It was also true in our department. In 1980 I'd come across precisely two other federalists at Justice. One was very crafty about hiding it; the other was Pierre Gauthier, who, like me, is not crafty at all and wore his Canadian heart on his sleeve. I would soon find out that there were many more of us than met the eye. Pierre, a former chief of staff to a minister in the first Bourassa government, was a senior administrator in the department. He and his family, like Catherine, Matt, and I, lived in Cap-Rouge. Pierre was very actively involved in organizing for the "No" side in the Québec City region. Pierre got me involved in getting people out to rallies, canvassing to locate potential "No" supporters, and other campaign-related activities. It was my first real taste of political organizing, and his depth of experience taught me a lot. The usual ban on political activity by civil servants (in force before the Charter ended the ban) had been lifted by the PQ government specifically for the referendum. Our next-door neighbour in Cap-Rouge, Claude Beausoleil, was also deeply involved in organizing, and through him I learned another important lesson: that participating actively meant a lot more than the old cliché about smoke-filled back rooms. You could hand out flyers. You could talk with your neighbours. I was amazed at how many of the people I spoke to planned to vote No in Québec City.

Meanwhile, within the civil service, known federalists were subject to teasing or to persistent attempts at "persuasion," which to some must have felt like intimidation. Others just kept their heads down. Not me. One day, an enterprising lawyer colleague, knowing that I planned to vote No, asked to have lunch with me, thinking he could beat it out of me during the course of the meal. Our deputy minister, René Dussault, was sitting right next to us in the cafeteria and couldn't help chuckling as he overheard our discussion, which must have sounded like something straight out of a re-education program. In fact, in the months leading up to the referendum the atmosphere was really difficult, and the cleavages it opened in the workplace, within families, and even between people who until then had been lifelong friends took many years to heal.

For me, the defining moment of the campaign was hearing Claude Ryan, the leader of the Québec Liberal Party, give a speech in a packed hall in Val-Bélair, a northern suburb of Québec City. As the director of *Le Devoir* from 1964 to 1978 he'd been Québec's leading public intellectual, writing immensely influential editorials and becoming known as *"le pape de la rue Saint-Sacrement"* ("the pope of the rue Saint-Sacrement," after the street in Old Montréal where the offices of *Le Devoir* were situated). In 1978, with the referendum on Québec sovereignty looming, he'd left the paper to run for the leadership of the Liberal Party. Now here he was, campaigning flat out for Canada. He had no voice left, but he was awe inspiring. His was an impassioned plea for reason, not to give up the country that our ancestors had built, that belonged to us, and that was so much a part of who we were. He took the referendum so much to heart that on the night of the vote, after the results were announced and showed a resounding 60 percent to 40 percent victory for our side, he couldn't let go and went on hectoring his opponents. It left him with an image problem that unfortunately stuck, but was completely at odds with the kind, caring, principled man that he was.

One of my biggest surprises of the 1980 referendum was that the vote confirmed what I'd been sensing on the ground, during the final weeks, working to convince the people I talked to of all that we stood to lose if we broke away from Canada. The Québec City region had voted No by a wide margin. Nevertheless, for many Québecers on both sides, the referendum was a deeply divisive, traumatic experience. The PQ government had lost decisively, and many who had supported the "Yes" side, including within the government, were hurting and bitter over the defeat. Within the civil service there were consequences. Québec City is a civil service town. Obviously, a great many government employees had voted No. Blaming them for the "Yes" side's loss in the provincial capital, the premier and his Cabinet spun around and trained their sights on the miscreants. As for me, in September I obtained my *titularisation* — that is, a permanent appointment to the civil service — and in the spring I was elected *Secrétaire de section* (section head) of the *Syndicat des professionnels du Gouvernement du Québec* (SPGQ), the Québec union of public service professionals and the second biggest union in the Québec government. I would have a front row seat as the re-elected PQ government started tearing up collective agreements.

When I got the call informing me that I had been recruited into the *Conseil de la langue française*, at first I thought it must have been a mistake. A federalist, whose first language was English, at the heart of the advisory body reporting directly to the Minister responsible for protecting and promoting the French language...?

When I sat down with Georges Rochon, the director of legal affairs and a former Jesuit (the president, Michel Plourde, had also left the priesthood but from a different order), I got straight to the point. "You're probably as thrilled to have me as I am to be sitting here, so maybe we can just move this along and I can apply to some other department," I said. To my surprise, Rochon, who turned out to be the nicest, most generous guy you'd ever want to meet, replied: *"Monsieur Mulcair, au contraire. J'aimerais tellement que vous veniez travailler avec nous"* ("Mr. Mulcair, on the contrary. I would love it if you would come and work with us"). When I asked him why, he said it was because in his shop everybody thought the same way, whereas he believed that people needed to realize that sometimes having another point of view was healthy and useful. He reiterated how pleased he would be if I accepted the offer, so I did, working under Camille Laurin, the minister of cultural development and author of Bill 101, the 1977 law introduced by the previous Lévesque government that established French as the language of work and as the sole official language in the province. Laurin had a brilliant mind and was incredibly structured and hard-working, qualities that he shared, as I was later to discover, with his party's nemesis, Claude Ryan, the man my dad had raved about years ago after seeing him give a speech in Toronto and who was later to become my mentor in the Québec Liberal Party.

During that time Catherine took courses and opened her own *institut d'esthétique* in Québec City. It was doing quite well, and she loved what she was doing, especially because it involved working with people. As for me, since my job in the civil service usually left me a little extra time during the day, I always had other things going. In the fall of 1979 I'd begun teaching Introduction to Law courses at the St. Lawrence campus of Champlain College, the English CÉGEP in Québec City, to the few English-speaking students from Québec City and a lot of French-speaking students who were there to soak up English. All of them were bright, hard-working, determined kids. Even if you weren't allowed to attend English elementary or high school under Bill 101, you could attend CÉGEP in English. I taught there for several years. I also gave some courses at St. Patrick's High School on Community and the Law and started teaching in the translation department at l'Université du Québec à Trois-Rivières (UQTR). Teaching was always a wonderful experience and, as every teacher knows, nothing is so rewarding as to run into a former student who thanks you for helping to steer him or her toward a good choice in their lives. This happened to me recently in Vancouver, when I ran into a student I had taught at St. Lawrence who was now, ahem, … a retired lawyer. You have to understand that when I was teaching him I was in my early twenties and he was in his late teens, so now he was in his mid-fifties and he was retired! It was very moving to me to hear him thank me for sparking his interest in the law.

In the spring of 1981, Matt turned three and Catherine's parents came to visit, as they did every year to celebrate his birthday. As for me, as *Secrétaire de section* of my public service union, I participated in a lot of discussions that were going on within the various departments in anticipation of what the government was going to do to us. For the moment, the PQ government appeared to want to let bygones be bygones, but 1981 was an election year and, given the setback they'd suffered in the referendum, we had every reason to be wary. That December in the provincial election, Québecers voted en masse to re-elect the government, giving the PQ a 49.3 percent share of their votes, an electoral peak the party has never matched since. Many observers outside Québec were shocked at this result, given that the province had voted decisively against the Parti Québécois's sovereignty-association project less than two years before. But Québecers were hedging their bets, as they often do, not unlike their neighbours in other provinces, most notably Ontarians, who tend to vote for one party at Queen's Park when another is in power in Ottawa.

By the summer of 1981 Catherine had acquired a faithful clientele, her business was doing very well, Matt was three and a half, and we decided to have another baby. Greg was born in the springtime, in perfect health, with a bilateral cleft palate and lip, a condition, the doctor explained, that was going to require close medical attention and repeated surgical operations. I will always remember holding him in my arms, just after his birth, as a kind nurse stood by. He looked right at me with those incredible eyes of his as I talked to him and reassured him. Catherine knew that getting him the best care had to become our number one priority; that determination of hers has always prevailed. Catherine sold her business to devote herself to the children full-time, and I went back to work, every day rushing to get home at night so that I could be with them. Until Greg's first operations, taking care of him was a full-time job. Both Catherine's parents and mine played a key role in ensuring that Greg did get the best care. The operations were an extraordinary success. Greg's personal tenacity is a reflection of those challenges he overcame.

Chapter Five
Learning the Ropes

With the election over, the re-elected PQ government brought out the steamroller against the civil servants. Early in the New Year the rumours began of a 20 percent pay cut across the board; the union prepared to defend its members. In the fall, the pay-cut legislation was tabled in the *Assemblée nationale* and we voted to walk out. It was a tough, raucous strike. On the first day there were arrests, and a close friend was roughed up in front of us as he was being arrested. The acrimony between us and the government was at its peak when we learned that the premier, René Lévesque himself, was going to be on Camil Samson's popular radio show. Our offices at 800 Place d'Youville happened to be in the same building as the radio station where Samson, a former parliamentary leader of the Parti Créditiste, a party promoting the social credit idea, had his studio. As the premier arrived, a donnybrook broke out between ourselves and his bodyguards. We were finally pushed aside and he was able to go in, but I went home to Cap-Rouge that night to find myself on the news among the strikers jostling the premier and to hear the astonishment in Catherine's voice as she said, *"Chéri, c'est toi? Mais qu'est-ce que tu fais là?"* ("Darling, is that you? But what are you doing there?")

While I was working at the *Conseil de la langue française*, I did a tour of the province's linguistic regions, during which I got a chance to meet a group of young leaders who had emerged in Québec's English-speaking community and come together to found Alliance Québec, a lobby group whose mission was to build bridges between linguistic communities in Québec and to defend the language rights of English-speaking Québecers. It included people like John Parisella (who had been chief organizer for the west of Québec during the 1980 referendum and was later to serve as chief of staff to Premiers Robert Bourassa and Daniel Johnson), Geoffrey Chambers (who had been John's assistant in the 1980 referendum and Alliance Québec's founding executive director), Eric Maldoff (who was president of Alliance Québec and went on to a stellar career in law), and Julius Grey (a constitutional and human rights lawyer who is now one of my closest advisers). They had been doing substantive work on problems that had arisen in the interpretation and implementation of certain provisions of Bill 101. We got on famously. I continued my work at the *Conseil de la langue française,* but as we were heading into the spring of 1983, it became clear that the government was going to go through with its planned legislation and the 20 percent cut to our salaries. When I told Michel Sparer, my friend and colleague at the *Conseil de la langue française,* that since my employer thought I was worth 20 percent less I saw no point in sticking around, he was shocked. "*Mais Tom, et ta permanence?*" he asked, referring to my job security as a civil servant. I simply replied, "*Ça n'existe pas, la permanence,*" meaning that nothing was permanent in life.

That summer, when Alliance Québec offered me a job as its director of legal affairs, the time had come to go. Catherine and I moved the family back to Montréal, and for the next two years I worked on cases for Alliance Québec, several of which concerned constitutional rights and made their way to the Supreme Court of Canada. We intervened in the Manitoba Reference on French language rights and again in support of the *Association canadienne-française de l'Ontario* (ACFO) in the court challenge it launched against the province of Ontario's Education Act, which eventually led to the Ontario Reference Case submitted by the province to the Ontario Court of Appeal. Both the Supreme Court and Ontario Court of Appeal decisions broadened the constitutional interpretation of the right to minority language education in Canada and had implications for French rights in Manitoba, New Brunswick, and across the country. I also handled the *Chaussures Brown's* case (known as *Ford v. Quebec*), in which the Supreme Court ultimately recognized a right to freedom of expression with regard to the language of commercial signs in Québec. Later in my career, at the request of Mr. Ryan, who no longer wished to use the "notwithstanding clause," I would go on to craft an honourable compromise on the language of commercial signs, with French predominant, that has never been contested twenty years on.

My time with Alliance Québec was incredibly stimulating. I learned a lot about management and about bringing communities together, about talking and listening to people, about trying to produce a result — in a word, about organizing. We worked flat out, almost around the clock, and the pace was crazy. I can remember going up to Québec City in the fall of 1983 to appear before a parliamentary committee. We'd put together a monster six-volume analysis in English and French, run off hundreds of copies, and loaded them into a rented truck that managed to break down on the way to Québec City. By the time it was finally back on the road we were running very far behind schedule. I had arrived ahead in Québec City, and I was pacing up and down the pavement in front of the *Assemblée nationale*, waiting for my friends to arrive, when I spotted a familiar figure coming up the street, trailed by a group of big strapping kids, just as the truck was pulling up. It was Sister Marianna O'Gallagher with her students from St. Patrick's High School. There were only six or eight minutes left before the parliamentary committee hearing was set to begin. What happened next was straight out of a movie. I asked Sister Marianna whether her students could give us a hand unloading the truck and carrying those hundreds of volumes to the committee room. "Boys, carry the books for Mr. Mulcair," she ordered, so that when, thanks to her, we marched into the committee room followed by the procession of students bearing the stacks of books, everyone thought it was an orchestrated stunt. Understandably, Gérald Godin, the PQ minister who was chairing the meeting, kept looking up and rolling his eyes, saying, *"Ben, ça suffit, là!"* ("Okay, that's enough!"). But far from having planned the whole thing, we were flying by the seat of our pants. Geoffrey Chambers gave the presentation in French that day. As for the text he was reading, the night before we'd had teams of secretaries typing it all night long in the hallway of the Hilton hotel across the street from the *Assemblée nationale* and in the morning running it off on the hotel photocopier. Marianna O'Gallagher was later to publish several historical works on the Irish in Québec. She was a dear friend.

Catherine, meanwhile, had begun a degree in education at the Université du Québec à Montréal (UQAM), and after a while she realized that the courses she most enjoyed were all related to psychology. She had always been a good listener and interested in people, from the clients at her business in Québec City to the kids she taught at École Saint-Léon-de-Westmount in Montréal. She applied to the Psychology Faculty and, despite the limited number of spaces, was accepted. After she obtained her Bachelor of Science in Psychology at UQAM, she transferred to the Université de Montréal for her master's degree, graduating in 1992. Throughout her full-time studies she not only held down the fort and took care of the kids during my numerous absences in Québec City, she also worked part-time in a long-term-care facility in one of the poorest parts of town. She has been practising psychology ever since and, in addition to her private practice, she works in long-term and palliative care. During the recent hearings on physician-assisted end-of-life care held in the *Assemblée nationale* in Québec City, Catherine was called to testify as an expert witness on behalf of the Québec Order of Psychologists. She has also served for many years on the regional health board of southwest Montréal.

Anyone who has worked as a community organizer will know how demanding it is, and with a young family you can operate in overdrive for only so long. Because the work I was doing then at Alliance Québec often kept me at the office until all hours, I was calling Catherine more and more often to say that I wouldn't be home for dinner. So, as much as I enjoyed the work at Alliance Québec, a short while later I handed in my resignation. When I got home and told Catherine I'd resigned, she went to the fridge and got out the bottle of champagne we were keeping for a special occasion, and we celebrated together. She was at university, I'd resigned my job, but we were happy. And that was all that mattered.

As luck would have it, just as I was ready to move on, a historic development took place in Manitoba. In June 1985, about a week after I left

Alliance Québec, the Supreme Court of Canada handed down its ruling recognizing the right of Franco-Manitobans to use their own language before the courts and declared invalid all four thousand existing provincial laws on the grounds that they were in English only. To avoid legal chaos, the ruling allowed Manitoba a very tight time frame to translate all the existing legislation.

To help translate its statutes, the Manitoba government hired a crack team of French-speaking lawyers from Québec, all of whom were impeccably bilingual. None of them, however, had studied British common law, and the province was looking for someone who was at once bilingual and trained in both branches of Canadian law to revise all the texts and make sure that, legally, they all said the same things in English and French. Thanks to my previous work with Michel Sparer I had gotten to know the director of legal translation, Greg Yost, quite well. My training and experience in translation opened the door, and I was immediately hired.

Having both civil and common law was a big advantage, and it has served me well throughout my career. But there's an added benefit, as well, because in law school at McGill we learned the comparative method, that is, to compare and contrast how the civil code and the British common law approach legal issues. Because we had professors who taught both, we developed the reflex of asking, "How did this other jurist arrive at that conclusion?" or, "I see the French civil code arrives at a different answer to this question than the British common law. Why?" What was so different in the French world view that led them to codify their laws, as opposed to the British system, which requires sifting through reams of jurisprudence to see what judges have ruled in similar cases? That kind of questioning became very much an integral part of my thinking. Today it helps me as party leader to better understand the different viewpoints of our caucus of MPs, who represent very different parts of Canada and don't think exactly alike on all the issues. The open-mindedness we were taught, that willingness and desire to hear out the other side of an argument, is also fundamentally, profoundly a Canadian value.

Canada was founded on accommodation between very different communities, which themselves could include large groups of people holding fiercely opposing views. For instance, the debate on whether Québec, then known as Lower Canada, should become an independent country or enter into a partnership with the three other colonies of Ontario (then Upper Canada), New Brunswick, and Nova Scotia, goes back to Confederation. Newfoundland's entry into the Canadian federation was similarly fraught with controversy, and it was ratified in a referendum by barely 50 percent of its population. Our country has long had its share of acrimonious debates that on rare occasions erupted into violence: the Rebellions in Upper and Lower Canada led by William Lyon Mackenzie and Louis-Joseph Papineau in 1837; the Red River and North-West Rebellions led by Louis Riel, leading to the creation of the province of Manitoba with guarantees of linguistic rights for French-Canadians — guarantees that were only now, a hundred years later, being so belatedly applied. In 1995, the result of the PQ-mandated second referendum on Québec independence was such a close call that in many other countries it might have degenerated into civil conflict. But that didn't happen. Why not? Maybe because on all of those occasions we kept talking, since we know in our heart of hearts that what we've got is worth keeping.

Canada's founding event was in fact a series of typically difficult, contentious conferences, held at Charlottetown and Québec City in 1864 and in London, England, in 1866, where our representatives aired their differences and the negotiations dragged on for days, repeatedly coming close to failing altogether. Even after the rise of a secessionist movement in a major part of the country, we mostly held fast to our democratic principles and twice (three times, if you count the 1992 Charlottetown referendum) allowed the issues to be resolved by the people themselves through public consultation. It's no accident that the words "peace, order, and good government" have become the motto that defines Canada's principles of governance. Foremost among these is "peace," the fundamental value that, until recently, had come to define us to others and that we promoted in other countries, everywhere in the world.

But let's not kid ourselves. Canada was never a foregone conclusion. We are a young country and still a work in progress. We are a nation of fixers who've never shrunk from the most difficult challenges. And a lot still needs fixing, including most urgently Canada's broken relationship with indigenous peoples. Sometimes getting it right takes us a long time, but we must never give up trying, and above all we must never trade away our values under any pretext. Especially not when it comes to protecting our rights and those of others.

Lately, we've been having a debate in this country about national security, and whether, to ensure the safety of Canadians, we need to give up some of our rights and freedoms. But none of us is or can be completely safe all the time. Security doesn't mean eliminating all risk. It's just not possible. Any one of us can die tomorrow, driving to work or crossing the street. Just as surely, a right or freedom can never be truly absolute. The constitutions of democratic countries do allow for restricting rights and freedoms in the public interest, but the burden of proof is squarely on the state, and the restriction must be minimal and must not exceed what is deemed reasonable in a free and democratic society. We must not allow ourselves to be scared out of our wits and bullied into putting at risk our democratic rights and freedoms by arguments based on fear and made for political gain, be it fear of terrorists or "murderers in your neighbourhood" — as one Conservative Party of Canada fundraising email warned. We are not engaged in a war against "one of the most dangerous enemies our world has ever faced," as Stephen Harper recently claimed in reference to ISIL, the Islamic State in Iraq and the Levant. Talk such as that, especially on the part of a sitting prime minister, is unconscionable and an affront to all those who served in two world wars, including my uncles, who must be rolling over in their graves.

It's simply not true that we have to choose between our safety and our freedoms, between having jobs or a clean environment, between our pocketbooks and the programs and institutions that we have built as Canadians. It's a deception, a false choice that serves the interests of those with power and influence, but not the country's interests, the public interest. When Stephen Harper decided to turn the Canadian economy on its ear in pursuit of his vision of making us into an "energy superpower," he bet the farm on resource extraction, thereby severely damaging this country's manufacturing sector, but he didn't have to. When he decided to gut environmental regulations, dismantle government bodies charged with oversight, muzzle scientists, and shut down research facilities across the country because their findings contradicted what he was telling Canadians, he didn't have to.

Now the market value of a barrel of oil has collapsed, throwing Canada's finances into turmoil, and Mr. Harper's economic plan is proving to be a short-sighted failure. Of course the price of oil will recover, but what was wrong-headed from the start was to make our economic prosperity, our financial solvency as a nation, so dependent on the price fluctuations of a single resource. A long-term economic vision would foster balanced growth across all sectors, placing the entire economy on more sound and stable footing. But that's the Harper method: always one or the other, never the whole.

Chapter Six
Go West, Young Man

When I was still studying law at McGill, I met a lot of students from western Canada who'd come to study in Montréal. They could have gone to any university, but they chose McGill because they wanted to understand what Québec was about, why people in the province felt the way they did, and why the politics were so different than in other parts of the country. In 1980 as a Québecer I had fought hard for Canada in the referendum, so in the early summer of 1985 the prospect of a job in Manitoba offered the opportunity to get to know another part of the country.

As soon as I got to Winnipeg my perspective changed dramatically. In Montréal, back then, you almost never saw an indigenous person. You knew there was a reserve just outside the city called Caughnawaga (now Kahnawake), and some people went there to play golf, but that was the full extent of your awareness. Now, as I went about my daily business, I was struck by the numbers of destitute indigenous people on the streets of Winnipeg. Many came in young from distant reserves in Northern Manitoba, drawn by the lure of the city, in search of work, but couldn't get hired. Too many fell prey to booze and drugs, with no way home. I'll never forget a group of kids, eight to ten years old, who were sitting on the sidewalk with a six-pack of Seven-Up and swilling their soft drinks, laughing, and spilling quite a bit over themselves. One of them asked another kid, "So what happens now?" His friend answered, "Now we stand up and we smash things." Whereupon they all got to their feet and began stomping on their Seven-Ups until they'd crushed the cans and sent them flying. They were pretending to be drunk. They were just kids, but they lived on the streets and they lived rough. There were areas of Winnipeg where you were told not to go, because there were large communities there that weren't able to integrate, where people survived however they could, living completely separate, segregated lives. It was shocking to me and deeply troubling to think that my country, Canada, a nation that prided itself on being the "good guy," tolerated injustice on that scale.

During my first six weeks out west, while I was working on the statutes, Catherine and the kids went to France to visit with her family. In the middle of August I was able to join them for a couple of weeks, and we had a nice holiday together. Afterward, for the next two years, I commuted, spending three weeks a month in Montréal revising the translation work and returning to Manitoba with stacks of translated material. One of the people I worked on the statutes with was Michel Sparer, who had been a colleague at the *Conseil de la langue française* and remains a dear friend to this day. A talented jurist and linguist, he brought to our task his expertise in legislative drafting and translation. Another extraordinary colleague from Manitoba who has become a lifelong friend is Michel Nantel. He went on to head the translation department and is one of the most prodigious translators I have ever met. Catherine and I have stayed in close contact with the Nantel family and are the proud godparents of their daughter.

Another big eye-opener for me happened in 1986 when the decision was taken in Ottawa to transfer the CF-18 (Canadian Forces fighter jet) maintenance contract from the winning bidder, Bristol Aerospace of Winnipeg, to Canadair in Montréal. Whenever I went back to Québec, people I talked to about it would shrug and say, "What's the big deal? Of course Canadair gets it. We've got the engineers, the technology, the plant. Ottawa should be able to award us the contract." But people in Winnipeg were beside themselves. It just wasn't fair, and fairness, I've always believed, is the foundation for justice.

The third realization that I took away also had to do with basic fairness. Before I got the job in Manitoba, while I was working in the Québec Justice Department, I'd heard vague stories that sounded like urban legend about francophone students in that province having to hide their textbooks whenever the inspectors came to their classrooms. But Greg Yost, who was in charge of the translation department when I arrived in Manitoba, told me it was all completely true. In the 1950s when he was growing up, the son of a French-Canadian mother, it was illegal to teach French in Manitoba, so when the inspector came around the teacher would tell them to hide their books on their laps under the desk. Greg is absolutely brilliant and one of the most well-read people I have met in my life. He is also a feisty, proud, right-wing conservative who, along with others, helped me to understand why many people in the West felt unfairly treated in the Canadian federation compared to people in the East, mainly Québec and Ontario. At the same time Yost was very open to Québec. He and his wife Jackie had lived in Montréal when they had first been married, and their five superlatively gifted children all grew up fluently bilingual. Greg understood the necessity of protecting French, not only the language but also the culture, in Québec and in the rest of Canada. Interestingly enough, he went on to run as a candidate for the Reform Party and wound up coming to Ottawa as Preston Manning's key constitutional adviser. We remain good friends.

In Manitoba, ground zero in the struggle for French rights was St. Boniface, a once thriving French Catholic parish that had been amalgamated into the city of Winnipeg. Founded by Roman Catholic missionaries in 1818, it had grown to acquire its own archbishop and had given itself a beautiful cathedral, a French university, and the first hospital in western Canada. The young Louis Riel had been educated there. The province of Manitoba had come into being as the result of a negotiation between the government of Canada and Riel's provisional Red River government, notably over the crucial question of French religious and linguistic rights. In 1870, Manitoba's entry into Confederation was enshrined in the Manitoba Act, which granted the new province legislative power over education while providing constitutional protection to religious and linguistic rights in the matter of education. Then, in 1890, as more and more English speakers arrived and settled in the province, the Manitoba government enacted legislation that removed funding for denominational schools, effectively negating the right of French-Canadians to be educated in their language — in other words, making it illegal. Another law also abolished French as an official language in the province. Both of these measures set off a furor in Québec, which had made the protection of French rights a bedrock condition of its entry into Confederation. For all these reasons the Manitoba schools question had remained a burning political issue and provided crucial historical context for understanding the battles over language in Québec. The French community in Manitoba had been fighting for its rights before the courts for more than a century. Now the Supreme Court of Canada had retroactively granted them redress, and that was why I was in Manitoba.

I had a lot of friends in St. Boniface, where the once vibrant French community was still grappling to hold on. The banks were bilingual, there were some signs in French, but the francophone population had shrunk considerably in proportion to the municipality's anglophone population, as more English speakers moved in and assimilation increased with each generation. Successive governments in Manitoba had remained steadfastly opposed to French linguistic rights. In fact, Sterling Lyon, the Conservative Manitoba premier, was still in office when my colleagues and I at Alliance Québec had intervened on the side of the Franco-Manitoban community in the Manitoba Reference Case. Lyon had even gone on the record defending his government's refusal to abide by its constitutional obligations to French-speaking Manitobans. These provisions, he argued, had been put in over a hundred years ago and were (quoting Shakespeare) "more honoured in the breach than in the observance." In addition, he claimed they were directive, not mandatory, so that applying them after all this time would be an improper and destabilizing intrusion into the province's practice.

Those statements by Sterling Lyon deserve to be given context. On December 13, 1979, as I was working away in the legislative drafting branch of the Québec Justice Department, we had gotten word of two Supreme Court of Canada decisions, one affirming language rights in Manitoba (the first of several Supreme Court rulings on this question), the other striking down key provisions in Bill 101 that dispensed with the obligation of legislating in English as well as French in Québec. Regarding Québec, the Court's decision stated that both versions of the statutes were equally authentic and that all steps of enactment had to be simultaneous, so that both versions of draft legislation had to be tabled and debated at the same time by the members of the *Assemblée nationale*. That very day, all of us in the legislative drafting branch got to work immediately. We worked around the clock and through that night. The *Assemblée nationale* sat until dawn re-enacting both versions of all of the legislation that had been adopted in French only, albeit with an unofficial English version, since the Lévesque government's first mandate.

So whereas in Québec the Supreme Court decision was taken seriously and acted upon immediately by René Lévesque's government, in Manitoba Sterling Lyon's government largely ignored it. For the next three and a half years, as the francophone community in Manitoba mobilized to try to get the government to do the right thing, the Lyon administration stalled and delayed, until in 1983 the government of Canada, in its *Reference re Manitoba Language Rights*, asked the Supreme Court to clarify whether the Manitoba government was constitutionally required to pass laws in both languages. By the time the Supreme Court rendered its historic decision on the Manitoba Reference two years later, it had taken ninety years for French-speaking Manitobans to have their constitutional right to have their province's laws in their own language affirmed. By contrast, Bill 101 was adopted on August 26, 1977, its unilingual provisions were struck down two years later, and all the legislation was enacted in English in a single night. Of course, it should be borne in mind that Québec's task was facilitated by the fact that an unofficial translation had been prepared for all legislation enacted after Bill 101, so as to be available in print. Re-enactment was therefore technically feasible, literally, overnight. Manitoba was facing the Herculean task of translating nearly a century's worth of legislation. In the event, tough negotiations with the interested parties led to a good-faith solution that required the translation of current statutes and regulations in a tight time frame. The mean-spiritedness that had characterized the approach of the Sterling Lyon Conservatives had, in the interim, been replaced with a more generous and open NDP government intent on finding a solution that was as fair and respectful as the people of Manitoba.

Anyone who believes in fairness can see from the above that Canadian history hasn't always been fair to French-speaking Canadians, who helped found this country and whose political leaders, civil servants, and diplomats have contributed so much to the fabric of the nation. French rights are bedrock Canadian values, and the need to affirm them is ongoing. As Opposition leader I fought hard to keep the old post office in St. Boniface and held the Harper government to account when it tried to cut the funding to *La Liberté*, the French-language newspaper in Manitoba. Recently, the French community in the Yukon has appealed·to the Supreme Court to have its right to French schools recognized. In Québec a company called TransCanada has consistently failed to submit to the National Energy Board in French, as well as English, all documents for the Energy East pipeline that is supposed to run through the province. The fight for French rights in Canada continues and merits the support of all Canadians.

I have very fond memories of Manitoba, which is one of the most beautiful places I know to visit. In late June, at the end of a full day's work, I could walk to my friend and colleague Michel Nantel's place in St. Boniface, get golf clubs, walk to the golf course, play eighteen holes, and still get back to my apartment hotel, the Place Louis Riel, in time to watch the sun set around 10:30 p.m. And Manitobans are wonderful people. Montréalers, as everyone who's been to the city knows, are notorious jaywalkers. The first time I walked across the street in Winnipeg, calculating the speed of the closest oncoming cars so as to get safely to the other side, I suddenly realized I'd stopped the traffic. When one of the drivers rolled down his window, I expected to be given a piece of his mind. Instead he asked me, "Are you all right, sir?" with a look of sincere concern. In that moment I learned that, whereas in Montréal you took your life in your hands when you crossed the street, in Manitoba people were so polite that the minute you stepped off the curb, they stopped to let you by.

Chapter Seven
Standing My Ground

In December 1987 Claude Ryan, as minister of higher education and science in the Liberal government of Robert Bourassa, named me president of the *Office des professions du Québec*, the government regulatory body charged with applying and enforcing professional and ethical standards as defined by the *Code des professions*, the framework legislation governing the forty-five professional orders in Québec. I'd first met Ryan during my time at Alliance Québec, but really got to know him in the spring of 1986, when the Québec government was in a spot of trouble over illegal schools. These were English Catholic schools that contravened Bill 101, the *Charte de la langue française*. Conflict was brewing, which Ryan resolved in typical fashion by bringing together everybody who knew the issue but came at it from different points of view, at eight o'clock on a Saturday morning. I'd been brought in by Jeff Polenz, an old friend from my days at Alliance Québec who was now a key political staffer for Mr. Ryan.

Around the table were senior lawyers, including brilliant litigators like Colin Irving, QC, who represented the English-speaking community in many legal cases, along with some senior civil servants from the Ministry of Education who I happened to know from my Québec City days. What ensued was a long, complicated discussion on very complex technical issues.

I expressed some ideas and made some recommendations, and maybe because I was young (thirty-one at the time), Mr. Ryan decided to show me who was boss. He waited until I'd finished speaking and, addressing himself to Colin Irving, said, "*Maître* Irving, we've just heard one point of view. Now could you kindly explain to us the actual situation?" To which Colin Irving, much to my delight, looked at Mr. Ryan and replied that he agreed completely with my analysis.

Mr. Ryan eventually named me to the *Commission d'appel sur la langue d'enseignement*. This was a tribunal that determined all the "cusp" cases regarding eligibility to attend English schools. It was good, hands-on training in a decision-making position, overseeing an important statute, listening to the people who came in to argue their cases, and it was a great experience. After two years we'd managed to clean up a messy situation on access to English schools and we'd provided advice on the illegal schools issue that Mr. Ryan found useful. In the middle of that process, the position of president of the *Office des professions* was vacated, and I was approached about taking it. It was a full deputy minister–level position, and a big step up for me.

Mr. Ryan invited me to his office on a Friday evening (he worked eighteen hours a day, seven days a week) to close the deal on the offer. I found him enjoying a cigar, a *péché mignon* (little indulgence) of his that very few people knew about. We had a very pleasant conversation. He saw my background at Justice as a big advantage and liked the work I had done at the *Commission d'appel sur la langue d'enseignement*. We agreed that I would start in early January. Having noticed on my curriculum vitae that I had just turned thirty-three, he remarked, "Ah! A highly appropriate age for the work you'll be doing." Ryan was a devout Catholic, so he was referring to the age Jesus was … when he was crucified! I got his hint that this was going to be a tough job.

As my predecessor's mandate had eight months left, it was stipulated in my contract that I would complete it, basically as a probation period, while Mr. Ryan kept a close watch on how I was doing. When the eight months were up he renewed my mandate for five years, but shortly thereafter he had to move on, because he was the premier's chief fixer and Mr. Bourassa kept giving him more and more responsibilities. After he was given another portfolio I saw him much less often.

The mandate of the *Office des professions* is to ensure that Québec's forty-five professional bodies are doing their job of protecting the public. For the next five years my role as president was to enforce legislation that regulated all of the professions — close to eight hundred regulations, representing one-third of government regulations in Québec — including the medical, legal, and technical bodies. Mr. Ryan had a strong desire to see positive reforms that enhanced public protection and the public interest. We opened up secretive disciplinary hearings to the public and the press. We got rid of fixed tariffs for fees that were being enforced in certain professions, and we stepped up our supervisory activities. As a sign that not everything was ready for change, I do remember the one time Mr. Ryan felt compelled to send a senior aide to find out whether I was serious in proposing to remove the "right" of pharmacists to sell cigarettes. The suggestion had come from the president of that profession, with whom I readily agreed ... to take tobacco out of pharmacies! It was a great idea whose time had not yet come. A few years later, of course, it was just common sense that pharmacies shouldn't be selling cigarettes, and the change went through without difficulty.

One of the key professions we regulated was that of medical doctors, who were then represented by the *Collège des médecins du Québec* (at the time called the *Corporation professionnelle des médecins du Québec*) and its president, Dr. Augustin Roy. The existing legislation provided inadequate mechanisms for patients to bring complaints against doctors. The events of the following months would lead to a major overhaul to enhance public protection.

In 1992 a series of complaints concerning allegations of sexual misconduct by doctors were brought to our attention at *l'Office*. It was clear to all of the members of *l'Office* that on this issue in particular, the *Collège* was not doing its job of protecting the public, and interventions by its president were the main reason. A complaint was brought to us involving a woman in Ottawa who alleged that she'd been sexually abused by a doctor in Montréal. That doctor's name had already come to our attention. Because of the seriousness of the allegations and the need to scrupulously protect the identity of the alleged victim, I asked to meet with her discreetly at her home after arranging for a person from a support group to be present. In the account she gave me she was very lucid and articulate in describing the abuse she had been subjected to while under the care of a psychiatrist, who had worked in Ottawa and at St. Mary's Hospital in Montréal. I launched an investigation and discovered that the man was a repeat offender. He always used the same modus operandi, a fact confirmed by another doctor who wouldn't go on the record. After the *Collège des médecins* got wind of our inquiries it began trying to thwart the investigation, and the case blew up in the media when it became clear that the *Collège* was dragging its feet. There were other cases as well, among them that of an orthopaedic surgeon who had a history of abusing children. At the time, the medical profession often dealt with its sexual offenders by moving them to a different location. In the end we managed to get the government to change the *Code des professions,* the professional standards and ethics code it imposed on all the professions. From then on, sexual misconduct by professionals was no longer tolerated: it was prohibited in law, period. More than a legislative reform, it was a change in culture.

However, my determination to protect the public, in this case women and children, by going after offenders and my unwillingness to back off had consequences. The issue had just become too hot, and the push-back that the government received from the professions was causing friction. I was offered the presidency of various other government agencies at the end of my mandate at *l'Office*, but I declined. I had stood on principle and thought I was doing a good job in my assigned role. So instead of accepting those offers, I decided to complete my term and return to private practice.

My term ended in August 1993, and I returned to working on my own, at home, and spending real quality time with Catherine and our two boys. I had several contracts with regulatory bodies in Canada and the United States and delivered numerous lectures on professional regulation. I also handled several legal cases involving the professions. But there was another reason that I was relieved to be closer to home and to my family.

During this period my dad's health took a turn for the worse. A top athlete in his youth, he had always been a big bear of a guy. Very tough and demanding, he often bellowed to be heard above our own roar. He was also brilliant and he loved to discuss and debate, often in very colourful terms. As he neared fifty he had been diagnosed with diabetes. His case was so severe that it led to many hospital stays. During his absences Mom, who was still teaching, began taking more and more care of his insurance brokerage. Later, my youngest brother, Sean, who was studying to obtain his professional licences, was able to ensure continuity of the family business.

Dad suffered a great deal but rarely complained. He went through several toe and then foot amputations and eventually lost both legs below the knee. It was tough on everyone, but of course toughest on him. When he had his car adapted, an old friend of his, Kevin Maguire, did something incredibly generous. He ploughed a dirt track for Dad from the driveway of the family home, which sits on the top of a steep hill, all the way around the property to the back door of my parents' room, which was at ground level. That way Dad could still get out and drive, which would have been impossible otherwise. His health slowly deteriorated until his final stay at Montreal General Hospital, when we all sensed that he was going to be leaving us soon. On what was to be his last St. Patrick's day, just a few weeks before his death, Catherine picked up a green top hat and some green balloons. When we got to Dad's room she produced a thimbleful of Bailey's. Dad cracked up. He just loved it. After he passed away we all asked Kevin Maguire to give the eulogy at Dad's funeral, because none of us was in a state to do it. He called everyone for anecdotes, and in the great Irish wake tradition he made sure that a touch of laughter lightened our tears as we accompanied Dad on his final journey. Canadian tenor John Mac Master, who is a childhood friend of mine, did us the kindness of flying in from an engagement far away to sing at the funeral. When his "Danny Boy" rang out just as my brothers and I were bearing the casket out of the church, we all were crying so much that one friend said we would have needed a canoe to carry us out of the door.

A bit before Dad's passing, the Québec Liberal Party had approached me to run in the next provincial election. Because my work at the *Office des professions* had been abundantly covered in the media, I had become a public figure, and the party thought my candidacy would attract attention throughout the province. Premier Robert Bourassa had retired in January

1994, after governing the province for nearly a decade and sacrificing his health during the Oka Crisis, when he fatally delayed the diagnosis and treatment of the malignant skin tumour that caused his death two years later. Daniel Johnson, son of the late Premier Daniel Johnson, had been chosen to replace him in January. In the post-Meech, post-Charlottetown atmosphere of the time, anti-federalist sentiment was at fever pitch. Lucien Bouchard's newly founded Bloc Québécois had just swept the province, winning 49.3 percent of the vote in the October 1993 federal elections; with fifty-four Québec seats in the House of Commons it catapulted to Official Opposition status in the Canadian Parliament. Provincially, Jacques Parizeau's Parti Québécois was comfortably ahead, enjoying support consistently above 50 percent in public opinion polls. The election was anything but a foregone conclusion.

The offer to run was serious. Catherine and I discussed it together, as we do all our decisions. Our love and respect for each other are such that whenever one of us is faced with an important choice, we talk it through, share our concerns, and, once the decision is made, offer each other unconditional support. As Catherine always says, loving another person means accompanying that person at every step along the path he or she chooses. I had been approached to run before, once in municipal politics and once at the provincial level, but the boys were young then and Catherine and I agreed that it was too soon. I still had a lot to learn and needed to gain much more experience before I could contemplate going into politics. Our time together was important. We've always considered it essential to keep in tune with one another, no matter the ups and downs of our daily lives. Even when I worked at the *Office des professions* and had to be in Québec City every week, I tried to be away no more than two days at a time. We still do our best to meet that standard — even today — as much as possible.

If the timing hadn't been right before, I had now gained experience in writing laws, in the machinery of government, in the many important ways in which good policy decisions could be used to redress wrongs and concretely improve people's lives, and in the positive impact of citizen activism on political decision making. Matt was nearly grown, Greg was already in high school, and both of our boys were very supportive. This time the stars seemed to align, but most of all I felt that I was ready. I told the party the answer was yes.

When it came to choosing a place to run, there was a lot of demand for the most winnable ridings. John Parisella was an old friend whom I'd replaced at Alliance Québec. He had been chief of staff to Premiers Robert Bourassa and Daniel Johnson and the director general of the Québec Liberal Party. John facilitated a discussion whose result was that Geoff Kelley, another friend whom the Party had recruited and who, like me, had worked and learned under Mr. Ryan, and I each ran in the riding that was the best fit. Geoff, who is a grandnephew of F.R. Scott and is now a minister in the Couillard government, ran in the West Island. I chose the riding where I grew up. In one of my very last conversations with Dad I told him I'd been asked to run in Chomedey. He was thrilled at the idea that I'd have the opportunity to represent the same area where he and Mom had raised their ten kids.

My 1994 election campaign was actually "two-for-one." Lise Bacon, one of the most highly regarded ministers in the Bourassa Cabinet, had stepped down shortly after Mr. Bourassa had resigned for health reasons. She went on to be named to the Senate by Jean Chrétien. In practical terms this meant that my campaign actually launched as a by-election to replace Mme Bacon as member of the *Assemblée nationale* for Chomedey. Daniel Johnson had told me he would coordinate the call for the general election to coincide with the by-election. Consequently, the by-election was automatically cancelled when the general election was called a month and a half later, but the net result was that I was in full campaign mode for several months.

I knew the riding well, and on my first day of door knocking I went back to our old house on 99th Avenue and walked my old *Gazette* delivery route! It was my first experience going door to door as a candidate, and I was lucky to be accompanied by Jeanine Papineau, an experienced volunteer who made it easy and fun. Jeanne Landry was another volunteer who was often by my side. She would go on to serve as my riding association president for the next thirteen years.

I soon learned that really good organizers (and my chief organizer, Jocelyne Roch, was simply the best) want the candidate out of their hair so that they can ... organize. So I was out campaigning on the ground seven days a week, going door to door, visiting every seniors' residence, every community group — and loving every minute of it. The riding was extremely diverse ethnically, culturally, and religiously. I attended religious services in at least a dozen houses of worship. Their sheer variety was an eye-opening crash course on one of Canada's defining characteristics: multicultural diversity.

I discovered that campaigning was hard work! Many people in the riding lived in triplexes, so I found myself running up and down stairs all day long. As I expected, the reaction to our message on the doorsteps was extremely positive. Many members of cultural communities in Chomedey had come to Canada to escape hardship and oppression in one form or another. Sophisticated voters, they understood that democratic values were shared by all — but they were, as a rule, unwilling to take a chance on anything that could compromise their prosperity or their children's rights as Canadians. Many seniors were leery of potential upheaval in their often fragile lives. The fact that Chomedey was a staunchly federalist riding was a big advantage that helped determine the favourable result.

Daniel Johnson ran a very solid campaign, but the *"alternance"* factor ("alternating" or "taking turns" in power) weighed heavily. Québec voters who wanted change after nearly a decade with one party in power had only one other party to vote for. The Parti Québécois won the majority of seats, and Jacques Parizeau, the premier elect, made no bones about where he was heading, promising a short, clear referendum question on Québec independence on a one-year horizon. For Chomedey voters, the choice was stark. I won my first election by a wide margin.

I set out to undertake the challenge of representing the people of my riding.

Chapter Eight
The 1995 Québec Referendum and Its Aftermath

In September 1994, when I was elected as the member of the *Assemblée nationale* for Chomedey, I shared an office with John Ciaccia, who had been a prominent minister in the Bourassa government. The Parti Québécois under Jacques Parizeau had just won the election, and now that John sat in the Opposition he was quietly heading toward retirement. He was a wise and wonderful guide to me as a parliamentarian. I was just coming off a very demanding mandate as president of the *Office des professions,* and I was used to giving no quarter. John Ciaccia taught me that "not every shot has to be a hardball to the head." Across the aisle was the PQ, which, with seventy-seven seats in the *Assemblée nationale* to the Liberals' forty-seven, had formed a majority government. Parizeau had campaigned on a promise to hold a referendum on Québec sovereignty within a year after taking power, and as soon as he came into office he signalled that he intended to keep his word. Now that the election was over, the battle was joined. I took to my new role with great relish, quickly earning the nickname of Opposition "pit bull" in the *Assemblée nationale.*

The referendum was set to be held a year after the provincial election, on October 30, 1995, with the campaign to last thirty days. The "No" side began with a comfortable lead in the polls. On September 17, during a speech in Saint-Joseph-de-Beauce, Jean Charest, the federal Conservative Party leader at the time, had scored a big hit when he'd brandished his passport and reminded Québecers of all the advantages of being Canadian, advantages they would lose, he warned, if they voted Yes in the referendum. The "Yes" side presented itself as *le camp du changement* (the side for change), but its numbers seemed flat. After the first week Parizeau decided to draft Lucien Bouchard, the Bloc Québécois leader of the Official Opposition in Parliament, to lead the "Yes" campaign, anointing him with the title of "chief negotiator for a sovereign Québec" in a proposed partnership with Canada. Bouchard left Ottawa at once and began criss-crossing the province, mesmerizing the crowds with his powerful oratory. On September 24, a prominent federalist named Claude Garcia, who was the president of Standard Life's operations in Canada, gave a speech during which he stated that defeating the "Yes" side wasn't enough, they had to be "crushed." Predictably, it caused an uproar. Within twenty-four hours, ads saying Québecers were tired of being "crushed" were on the air all over the province.

Five years earlier, in 1990, Lucien Bouchard's dramatic resignation from the Mulroney Cabinet and his defection from the Conservative government to protest the rejection by "English Canada" of the "distinct society" clause in the Meech Lake Accord had won him the adulation of nationalist Québecers, angered by what they saw as a rejection of Québec by the rest of Canada. His decision to found the Bloc Québécois as a federal outgrowth of the Parti Québécois had turned Canadian federalism on its head and sent shock waves through the corridors of power. Bouchard was a superlative orator and a highly respected lawyer, but his stature was about to rise even more. In December 1994, with a PQ government newly ensconced in Québec City and a referendum on sovereignty less than a year away, Bouchard had contracted flesh-eating disease. The entire province had held its breath while doctors raced against the clock to save him as his life hung in the balance. Having lost his leg and made a heroic recovery, Bouchard had achieved almost sainted status. Now his person took on a messianic aura, and his rallies unfolded in an atmosphere of quasi-religious fervour.

I'll never forget door-knocking in an area of my riding, L'Abord-à-Plouffe, where I'd won a large majority of the votes in the recent provincial election. A lovely senior woman smiled and said, *"Monsieur Mulcair, j'ai voté pour vous et je le ferai encore, mais Monsieur Bouchard a tellement souffert pour nous!"* ("Mr. Mulcair, I voted for you and I will vote for you again, but Mr. Bouchard has suffered so much for us!"). At the same time, many "soft nationalist" voters saw him as a reassuring presence who would work to preserve Québec's ties with Canada, in the tradition of René Lévesque and his vision of sovereignty-association. Parizeau, meanwhile, had other ideas, which, as Chantal Hébert and Jean Lapierre's book, *The Morning After*, reveals, he wasn't sharing with his "chief negotiator." Far from offering to negotiate, he planned to declare unilateral independence immediately after a referendum victory, no matter how slim the margin of victory.

During the campaign, Montréal was ground zero for the "Yes" and "No" camps. Emotions ran high. Jacques Parizeau's Parti Québécois government had thrown every asset possible into promoting the sovereignist cause. Scores of Québec's biggest stars, from popular singers, songwriters, and film and television actors to writers, poets, and other artists, weighed in supporting the grand design. Meanwhile, public resources were mobilized in unprecedented ways to promote the cause of both the "Yes" and the "No" camps. On the "No" side, federal and provincial politicians, aware they were sitting on a powder keg, appeared out of ideas and paralyzed. The "No" Committee, chaired by Daniel Johnson, included representatives of the federal parties. The federal Liberals, who were in power in Ottawa, were resented and distrusted ever since the failure of the Meech Lake Accord, which had sought to enshrine the recognition of Québec as a distinct society in the Constitution and which Pierre Trudeau and many federal Liberals had ferociously opposed.

Right from the start, while the "Yes" camp showed imagination and spoke in the language of symbols that sought to inspire, the "No" Committee cranked out soulless formulas and economic arguments that seemed deliberately drained of emotional content. Even before the campaign began, the decision to trot out some of Québec's top business leaders and CEOs to line up in support of remaining in Canada had given the "Yes" camp an opening to call the "No" side *le camp des milliardaires* (the billionaires' camp).

During that time I worked closely with my old friend Geoffrey Chambers, who by then was vice-president of the Québec Liberal Party and a member of the official "No" committee. I and my fellow Opposition members of the *Assemblée nationale* were designated spokespersons for the "No" campaign and had been asked to hold town hall meetings in our various ridings around the province. We drove wherever people would give us a hearing, and their anxiety was palpable. The problem for us was that nobody could say what would happen in the event that the "Yes" side won. The Parti Québécois government had unilaterally claimed sole authorship of the referendum question by passing a law in the *Assemblée nationale*. The wording of the question ("Do you agree that Quebec should become sovereign after having made a formal offer to Canada for a new economic and political partnership within the scope of the bill respecting the future of Quebec and of the agreement signed on June 12, 1995?") was complicated and could be interpreted in many different ways. Furthermore, no prior agreement had been reached, let alone discussed, between the Québec government and the government of Canada on what would come next if the "Yes" side won. What percentage constituted a mandate, and what would such a mandate empower the parties to do — or not? No one really had a clue except the Québec premier, Jacques Parizeau.

I'll never forget a conversation with the service representative at my local Ford dealership in Chomedey where I'd taken my van for a repair. It was just a few days before the referendum. He hopped in with me to see if everything was okay, and we drove for a few minutes on Autoroute 440. He knew that I was the local MNA and, after some chit-chat, he turned to me and said, *"Vous savez, après nous avoir dit Non avec Meech, si nous votons Non, ils vont penser qu'on est des ti-counes."* ("You know, after they said no to us on Meech, if we vote No, they'll think we're a bunch of pushovers.") He was referring to the rejection of the Meech Lake Accord in the "rest of Canada." What that man was telling me encapsulated the whole campaign. Everyone had their own interpretation of what was going to happen and what it would mean. And that was precisely the problem.

The NDP's position is clearly set out in the Sherbrooke Declaration adopted by the party in 2006. Not only is our position the norm for all public consultations in democratic countries, including in elections, referendums, and plebiscites, but it's also based on common sense. Consider for a moment that a hypothetical future referendum were to be won for the "Yes" by 50.58 percent, the margin of victory eked out by the "No" in 1995. Does anyone think that such a result would give the sovereignist leaders anything more than a very weak mandate? At the same time, randomly insisting on a margin of 60 or 65 percent *only for the "Yes" side,* as some have suggested, is not only unrealistic and dishonest but demonstrably unfair and disrespectful of people's democratic rights. One side is essentially telling the other, "If we get over 50 percent we win, but if you get over 50 percent— or anything less than 60 or 65 percent — we still win." A classic case of "Heads I win, tails you lose." Apparently the British, when they were preparing to face a Scottish referendum, took only a few months to figure that out.

You can't respect the democratic process only when it suits you. Above all, you have to respect the voters. Once again, it all comes back to fairness. Voters who feel disrespected, voters who feel the game is rigged against them, are quick to anger — and an angry electorate is not inclined to reason. Besides, by setting the bar any higher than 50 percent + 1, the Canadian government would be setting a trap for itself. If Yes doesn't mean Yes, but instead means something like "Maybe now you'll understand how angry we are," then for a lot of people there is no longer any reason *not* to vote Yes to a sovereignty question. On something as grave as the future of Canada, Yes had to mean Yes, not "if," "but," or "maybe." We're not dealing with a strike vote, designed to pressure an employer into agreeing to a new collective agreement. People have to understand that a Yes result changes everything and brings with it uncertainty and turmoil.

Leaving the lure out in the country that it would require a super-majority as high as 60 or 65 percent for Québec to secede would encourage voters to believe that they could use their vote to "send a message," to show that Québec couldn't be messed with, and maybe force the feds to offer a better deal. But even with such a rule imposed by Ottawa, if the "Yes" side won with, say, 58 percent, you can bet that sovereignist leaders would interpret it as a mandate to separate and act accordingly. Which is when all hell would break loose for the country. One of the worst mistakes we can make is to deceive the voters into thinking that by voting Yes they are voting for something else. Some say it would be unthinkable to let the country break up on a vote of 50 percent + 1. I say it would be unconscionable to let our relationships as Canadians degenerate that far.

In the spring of 2014, in my capacity as leader of the Official Opposition, I received a visit from representatives of the Scottish Office of the British Parliament who knew I'd fought for the "No" side in both of Québec's sovereignty referendums and wanted to consult with me on the upcoming Scottish referendum. I explained that one of the things I'd always fought for was to improve the lives of working people and quoted Québec Premier Pauline Marois, who'd famously mused that if Québecers voted to separate from Canada, there would be "years of upheaval" (*"des années de turbulences"*). "How," I asked them, "will creating years of upheaval enhance the lives of average working families?" I added that in this whole debate what I'd always seen was a battle of élites. My visitors replied that I had just given arguments very similar to those of Scottish Labour in their debates with the Scottish National Party. The British and Scottish governments later held talks for the purpose of hammering out mutually agreed terms, including the wording of the question to be submitted to voters and the precise percentage of votes that would constitute a win. Agreement was reached on the question "Should Scotland be an independent country?" and the British government declared that if a simple majority (50 percent + 1) of votes cast were in favour of independence, "Scotland would become an independent country after a process of negotiations." The Scottish referendum of 2014 set the standard for democratic consultations. The question must be mutually agreed by the parties, and the side that wins, wins, no matter how heartbreaking for either side.

As the weeks went by that fall in 1995, the sovereignist camp kept gaining in support. By mid-October some public opinion polls put the "Yes" in majority territory. In the final week, as the date of the vote drew near, the federal politicians in Ottawa, who'd reluctantly agreed to keep a low profile, lost patience. A big rally was hastily planned with Prime Minister Chrétien, during which Jean Charest gave an impassioned speech, again brandishing his Canadian passport as a symbol of all that would be lost if the "Yes" side won. On October 24, six days before the vote, the Grand Council of the Crees of James Bay, which had publicly challenged the sovereignist camp's contention that the Crees and their territory would, as a matter of course, be included in a sovereign Québec, organized their own, separate referendum. The move attracted little notice, but the Cree referendum, which took place in the middle of the fall goose hunt, required an extraordinary level of organization. As hunters streamed in from the bush to vote, voter participation reached 77 percent, an astonishing number considering the low average turnout of indigenous Canadians in federal and provincial elections.

The question they voted on was unequivocal: "Do you consent, as a people, that the Government of Quebec separate the James Bay Crees and Cree traditional territory from Canada in the event of a Yes vote in the Quebec referendum?" The Inuit of Nunavik in Northern Québec also held their own referendum, asking the question: "Do you agree that Quebec should become sovereign?" When those results were tallied, the Crees and Inuit had voted No by a whopping 96.3 percent and 96 percent, respectively.

The most memorable event of the final days was without a doubt the *grande manifestation de l'amour:* the Unity Rally at the Place du Canada in Montréal, three days before the referendum vote. That day thousands of Canadians jumped in their cars, boarded trains, or flew in from all over the country, some from as far away as Vancouver and St. John's, to gather and plead with Québecers to stay in Canada. Catherine and I waited for the boys to arrive in commuter trains. All their classmates were heading to the rally. The huge, televised event was immediately decried by supporters of the "Yes" side, who denounced the bargain-basement prices offered by the airlines, the time off granted by employers, the chartered buses arranged at the behest of federal Liberal Cabinet minister Brian Tobin to help bring people in from Ontario. The whole operation, in their eyes, was illegal because its costs couldn't be tabulated and contravened the spending limits set for each side by Québec's referendum law. But the sincerity of that outreach to Québecers by so many of their fellow Canadians was real, and the anguish it expressed reflected the powerlessness we all felt, on the eve of an event that concerned everyone, inside and outside Québec, and that risked changing all our lives in profound, unknowable ways. The fact is that none of our leaders, on either the "Yes" or the "No" side, had levelled with us on what they would do if the unthinkable, or the dream, depending on which side you were on, actually came to pass.

And as we all know, it very nearly did. On referendum night, the "No" side's hair-raising, near-death victory by a margin of 0.58 percent — so close, in fact, to the 50 percent + 1 that was later to be dismissed as a "clear result" by the Liberal Party of Canada — stunned the country and left a bitter aftertaste, even among the winners. Accusations flew on both sides. Jacques Parizeau's outburst on the night of the vote, blaming "money and ethnic votes" for the "Yes" camp's defeat, shocked many people. In my own heavily multicultural and federalist riding of Chomedey, 5,426 ballots had been rejected by government scrutineers. Despite my own best efforts as the MNA for Chomedey, that strange anomaly was never thoroughly investigated or properly prosecuted. On the tenth anniversary of the referendum, I published an article entitled *"Les dix ans du référendum"* ("Ten Years After the Referendum"), recapitulating the whole sordid affair.

Jacques Parizeau had always said that he would resign if the "No" side won. He stepped down the next day, and Lucien Bouchard, after resigning his seat in Parliament, replaced him as leader of the Parti Québécois on January 27, 1996. He was sworn in as premier two days later. Having lost the referendum by such a razor-thin margin, many sovereignists began spoiling for a rematch. In response, Bouchard declared that a third referendum would not be held unless the "winning conditions" could be assembled, the first and foremost of which was a balanced budget. Bouchard embarked on a mission to eliminate the deficit by instituting drastic reductions in government spending and draconian cuts in service, particularly in the health sector, that shocked and alarmed his supporters. Then in July the first of two weather-related natural disasters that were to mark Bouchard's time in office cast him in the role of statesman. For two days, torrential rains pounded the Saguenay–Lac-Saint-Jean region. Rivers burst their banks, sweeping away everything in their path, ripping apart homes, and burying cars under oceans of mud. It was the worst flood ever recorded in the province's history. It left six dead, caused the evacuation of 16,000 people, and wreaked havoc over a vast area stretching from Tadoussac all the way north to Chicoutimi and east to Sept-Îles. When it was over, the damage was estimated at $1.5 billion. Bouchard and Prime Minister Chrétien collaborated in providing emergency aid to the affected areas; later, a commission of inquiry instituted by the premier recommended tighter regulation of hydroelectric dam construction and that each municipality in Québec develop a plan for dealing with major emergencies. The 1996 *"déluge du Saguenay,"* like the catastrophic Alberta floods in 2013, brought out the very best in our leaders by calling on them to embody, by their actions, the most profound of Canadian values, the one that our country was founded on and that continues to define us, the people of this vibrant, unbelievably diverse, resilient federation, from coast to coast to coast: the bedrock Canadian value of solidarity.

Chapter Nine
Changing of the Guard

The ice storm that struck Québec in January 1998 was a defining moment for Lucien Bouchard, whose performance as premier during the crisis made him more popular than ever. It also marked one of the most difficult challenges Daniel Johnson had faced as leader of the Opposition and of the Québec Liberal Party. Daniel had been leader since briefly replacing the ailing Robert Bourassa as premier in 1994, just months before I became a candidate to run in my old hometown of Chomedey. Daniel had been one of the strongest ministers in the Bourassa government, and his organizers had done such a phenomenal job of sewing up support for his leadership that no one had run against him. Though Johnson was brilliant, strong-willed and a highly competent manager, his public persona — so different from the engaging, witty colleague with the spectacular sense of humour he was in private — was that of someone detached from the concerns of ordinary folk. An intellectual with sterling academic credentials, he'd come into politics with an unmatchable pedigree. His father, Daniel Johnson senior, had been a Cabinet minister under Maurice Duplessis, whom he had succeeded as leader of the Union Nationale and then premier of Québec from 1966 until his untimely death two years later, while still in office. Daniel Johnson senior had also written a book, *Égalité ou indépen-*

dance, in which he made the case for "independence if necessary, but not necessarily independence," paraphrasing Prime Minister Mackenzie King's famous "not necessarily conscription, but conscription if necessary," spoken during the Second World War. Both of Daniel Johnson's sons went on to be premiers of Québec. Daniel Johnson junior's brother, Pierre-Marc, who was a medical doctor and a lawyer, became premier after succeeding René Lévesque. Daniel (junior)'s wife, Suzanne Marcil, was a successful businesswoman who was very well liked. She was often by his side. During the 1998 ice storm, as Opposition leader, Daniel decided, quite correctly in my opinion, to keep a low profile. What was a heartfelt attempt to avoid grandstanding during the disaster was instead portrayed in the media as a lack of compassion or concern.

Shortly thereafter I joined some of my colleagues in the *Assemblée nationale* travelling to Toronto to play in a friendly hockey tournament against a team of Ontario members of the Provincial Parliament. Jim Flaherty, then a provincial minister, was on that team, and he was still a very good hockey player. I was on my way to supper at my sister Maureen's, who by then was living in Toronto, when I got an unexpected call from Georges Farrah, our party whip in Québec City. Another colleague, Robert Middlemiss, had been scheduled to travel to a Commonwealth conference in London, and Georges wanted to know if I could take his place. It was a plum offer and I really wanted to accept. It meant being away from Catherine and the boys for longer than usual, but we agreed and I returned to Montréal to pack my bags in preparation for my flight the following Tuesday. The day before I was due to leave, I went to the riding office. While I was getting briefed on the conference I was being sent to attend, Jocelyne Roch, my very experienced riding assistant, came in to say I had an emergency call from deputy whip Norman MacMillan. Norm was one of the most loyal people you'd want to meet, and he was devastated because he'd been tasked with phoning a list of MNAs to tell them that Daniel Johnson was about to resign as leader of our party. As for me, I was leaving for London the next day. Any involvement I might have in deciding who Daniel's successor was going to be would have to take place from the other side of the Atlantic.

I spoke at length with Pierre Paradis, who was House leader and a Jedi master of political gamesmanship in the *Assemblée nationale*. He and I were close and were similarly tasked with taking on the PQ government in the *Assemblée nationale*. Because Pierre had run for the leadership in 1983, narrowly edging Daniel Johnson for second place in the race that had marked Robert Bourassa's return to the helm of the Québec Liberal Party, I had always assumed that he would take another kick at the can if the opportunity came again. But there was clearly a very strong force pushing him away from any such thoughts. In the end, Pierre chose not to run because it quickly became very clear that Jean Charest was the prohibitive choice. Charest was the leader of the federal Progressive Conservative Party, which had been reduced to two seats in the 1993 general election. Despite the unprecedented defeat inflicted on his party, Charest himself remained popular, and his stellar performance for the "No" side during the 1995 referendum campaign had made him the darling of the federalist base of the Québec Liberal Party. After months of pressure from Québec Liberals to switch over to provincial politics, he had agreed to accept the leadership on condition that no leadership race would be held.

On the night of the party leadership convention, which was held at the Palladium in Québec City, Jean Charest was chosen by acclamation. I'd gotten to know Jean Charest during the 1995 referendum campaign and, as a newly minted MNA working my hardest in the battle to save Canada, I had been just as impressed as everyone else by the skill and passion with which he made his case. Charest gave it his all and was credited with helping to tip the balance for the "No" with his passport speech. He was a very talented politician.

In the Québec election that followed in November 1998, the PQ won more seats than the Liberals, who nevertheless garnered a higher percentage of the vote. What explains this result is that the PQ's support was distributed much more efficiently among the province's ridings than ours. My riding of Chomedey included a very large population of Greek origin. I got to know and appreciate the volunteers and community leaders with whom we worked on a regular basis, in particular Spiros Roumbas and his wife Niki. After the 1998 election I attended one of those great after-Mass lunches that were put on by the Women's Auxiliary of St. Nicholas Church. Watching them set out the meal for the hundreds of people packed into the basement of the church always amazed me. I admired their organization as .

they formed up in a line and handed everything out in a matter of minutes. I used to tell them that they should be the ones running the government, and I was only half joking.

On that particular Sunday I had a memorable conversation with the erudite parish priest, Pater Vasilios, who was one of my favourite personalities in the Greek community. I still remember it as if it were yesterday. Pater Vasilios was upset because the PQ had been returned to power despite having won fewer votes than the Liberals. "What is this system, Mr. Mulcair, where you win but the other party gets to form the government?" he asked. I did my best to explain the British parliamentary system, but Pater Vasilios was having none of it. "The British, they know NOTHING about democracy. The Greeks invented democracy. Change this system, Mr. Mulcair." That lively exchange comes back to me every time I explain the NDP's plan to bring in proportional representation.

Shortly after that election, Jean Charest, newly minted as leader of the Opposition in the *Assemblée nationale*, began putting together his inner circle. He tapped the highly experienced Pierre Paradis as his House leader and, much to my surprise, appointed me Deputy House leader. Charest had been through rough-and-tumble times in Ottawa. He'd seen what a strong, structured Opposition had been able to do to Brian Mulroney's Progressive Conservative government, and he wanted us to be a solid, forceful, and determined Opposition. We'd gotten to know each other by then, and he'd seen that I didn't back down from a fight. He too was Québec Irish, on his mother's side, and enjoyed a good scrap, but he also understood that he must now be seen as a premier in waiting. We didn't disappoint. Through sheer hard work, acting as a structured, disciplined Opposition, we got the better of our tough, seasoned opponents in the PQ government.

Chapter Ten
Forming the Government

On the night of April 14, 2003, I was re-elected in my riding of Chomedey, and the Québec Liberal Party swept to power with seventy-six seats. The Parti Québécois was reduced to forty-five seats and its vote share shrank to 33 percent, a ten-point drop since the previous election. Jean Charest was now premier of Québec, and his first order of business was forming a Cabinet.

My in-laws were visiting from France, as they often did at that time of year, because Catherine, Matt, and Greg all have their birthdays within the same couple of weeks. The election had taken place just over a week earlier. I was hopeful about being asked to be a member of the Cabinet but, having no previous experience in forming a government, I was finding the wait excruciatingly long. Then the call came. Catherine and I were in the car with her parents and the kids, coming home from a birthday meal. I signalled to Catherine to pull over so I wouldn't lose the signal. My heart was pounding as Hugo d'Amours, one of Charest's close advisers and one of those bright young people you get to meet in politics, stated the purpose of his call. After years in Opposition I was being asked to come later that night to a downtown hotel to meet with Mr. Charest himself. I knew what it meant.

Once inside the hotel I found that events were scripted to a T. I saw one or two colleagues, but no one else, as our visits were staggered. There was a whole process for sending different people to different floors and having them wait in different rooms. One of the first who came in to see me was the party president, along with a senior organizer. He gave me no hint as to the portfolio I would be offered but told me my chief of staff was going to be a fellow named Alain Gaul, saying he was a young lawyer from the Gaspé. I'd never heard of Alain Gaul. I tried to push for Jocelyne Roch, my highly competent, long-time riding assistant, who'd not only done two terms with me but had also completed two full mandates with another MNA during the Liberals' previous spell in power. Nothing doing: they were going to control the chiefs of staff. The next meeting came as a very pleasant surprise. I was taken to another floor to meet the person who'd been tasked with doing the final vetting. That person was Daniel Johnson. I learned a lot, there and then, about Jean Charest's method of keeping everyone on board. It was a very smart move.

The third and final interview was with Mr. Charest himself and his new chief of staff, Michel Crête, a very experienced gentleman whom I'd heard of but didn't personally know. Mr. Charest told me he'd be naming me minister of the environment. A detailed mandate letter, setting out expectations regarding policy and deportment, was presented to me for my signature. The premier-elect explained that in our new government, the Ministry of Sustainable Development, Environment and Parks was going to play a major role and that the environment portfolio would be considered as an economic file. I was thrilled. Environment had been Jean Charest's portfolio in Prime Minister Brian Mulroney's government. As minister of the environment, Charest had led the Canadian delegation to the Earth Summit, the United Nations Conference on Environment and Development, held in Rio de Janeiro in 1992. Evidently, the environment file was close to the premier's heart, and I would presumably be given the leeway to get a lot done. I hurried downstairs to find Catherine, who was discreetly parked around the corner at some distance from the hotel. When I told her what had happened, her eyes filled with tears of joy. She was so moved and happy for me. "You've earned this," she said. "You've worked so hard for so many years."

On the day of my swearing in, in Québec City, I was introduced to my first bodyguard, Julien Brousseau. The bodyguards were constables in the Public Security Ministry, specifically trained for the task of protecting Cabinet members. They were top-notch, they were armed, and they were with us at all times. The whole family grew very close to them over the next three years. When we first got into the car with Julien Brousseau, shortly after the swearing in, I sat beside him in the front while Catherine, Greg, and my mom got into the back of the vehicle. Matt was driving Jasmyne and Catherine's parents in his own car. I hopped into the minister's limousine, looked at Julien, and told him we were going home. He gave me a blank look with a half-smile. Of course, he had no idea where that was. Then he saw Catherine chuckling in the rear-view mirror and couldn't help laughing. We then directed him to our house. Years later, after I'd left the Cabinet, he and his wife Francine stopped by our place in Beaconsfield on their way to Dorval Airport, and he opened up about that day. As it turns out, I had a bit of a reputation for being very tough on the ministers of the previous PQ governments. That characterization had made its way to the bodyguards, who were somewhat wary. After Catherine took to calling him "*Monsieur* Julien," it didn't take long before he became part of the family. He remains a dear friend to this day. The other bodyguard permanently assigned to me was François Morris. He began working for me a couple of months into the mandate. He was younger than Monsieur Julien and strong as an ox, but just as professional. Events would lead to his also becoming a lifelong family friend.

For while there were many very rewarding moments during my time as Québec minister of the environment, that period wasn't devoid of tragedy. One evening, in 2005, as I was attending a meeting of the priorities committee of Cabinet in Québec City, Jacques Dupuis, the minister of public security, came in and said that three of our bodyguards had just been in a terrible accident. After parking their cars, they had begun crossing the Grande Allée on their way to have supper when a car hit them. Two of the bodyguards were lightly injured, but François, my bodyguard, had suffered horrific multiple fractures to his skull and other serious injuries.

I rushed to the hospital. His wife Nancy jumped in her car and drove in from the South Shore of Montréal, where they lived. François's father arrived and was horribly shaken at the sight of his son, who was then in his late twenties. It was touch-and-go for several days, but François was incredibly fit. That level of fitness, added to his tremendous willpower, no doubt combined to help him recover as well as he did in the end. Nevertheless, he lay in a coma for some time. He received excellent care at Saint-François d'Assise Hospital in Québec City. From the moment he was brought in, he was put in the hands of an extremely capable young neurosurgeon who said he was going to pull through, and he did. Catherine and I visited him often in Québec City and later in Montréal, after he was transferred to be close to his wife. We have stayed close ever since.

When I met Alain Gaul, the new chief of staff who had been assigned to me, I didn't beat around the bush. "You weren't my first choice," I told him. He didn't miss a beat. "Neither were you mine," he shot back. I knew instantly that we were going to get along. Today he is once again my chief of staff as leader of the Official Opposition in Parliament.

Chantale Turgeon had just completed her studies in communications at the Université de Montréal when a friend who was already working on my campaign suggested she try volunteering for my election as well. She proved such an asset to my campaign that, once elected, I went on to hire her as my press secretary in Québec City. She was extraordinarily efficient and had a phenomenal flair for giving the right advice when I needed it most. She is now my deputy chief of staff.

Being named to the Cabinet meant that I now had to have two offices, the minister's office in Québec City and the riding office in Chomedey. My riding assistant, Jocelyne Roch, had been offered a job in the premier's office. Since I could no longer be as present in the riding as I had been, I needed someone I knew well, someone I could trust to be my alter ego and serve as a crucial link between my constituents and me as their representative. Graham Carpenter had been my younger brother Sean's best friend since childhood. I'd watched him grow up. I asked Julien to drive me up to Sainte-Anne-des-Lacs where Graham lived and found him chopping wood outside his father's house. He couldn't understand why I'd thought of him but accepted without question and went to work immediately. He still does a magnificent job of running my office in Outremont.

That first summer as environment minister, I was taking a couple of days off with Catherine in upstate Vermont when I got word of the department's growing concern for a journalist who was on a hunger strike to protest the proliferation of blue-green algae in Missisquoi Bay at the top of Lake Champlain. Blue-green algae is the non-scientific name of cyanobacteria, one of the oldest life forms on Earth. When fed nutrients from septic or agricultural runoff, they can cause massive algal blooms in lakes, depleting the oxygen in the water and making it impossible for other life forms to survive. They are also harmful to animals or humans who drink the water.

The journalist, whose name was Robert Galbraith, had resisted all attempts by his family to dissuade him from his fast and seemed determined to pursue it to the bitter end. He had recently returned from covering the war in Iraq and he was having a tough time. Sensing the gravity of the situation, Catherine urged me to return to Canada immediately, to go to the man's house, to try to meet with him, and to offer my support to him and his family. So we packed up and drove across the border to the man's house, where our bodyguard François came to meet us. Catherine and I spent a good part of the afternoon with the journalist and his wife, and other family and friends. We walked to Missisquoi Bay, not far from his house. The blue-green algae were in full, toxic bloom. The antiquated septic systems of many waterfront homes and agricultural runoff from nearby farms were the main sources of the contamination. After talking a long while, and despite my hesitation at appearing to act under threat, Mr. Galbraith was persuaded to end his hunger strike on the clear understanding that we would be announcing a plan to deal with the problem.

Protecting wetlands and filtering marshes had long been a priority for the environmental protection legislation of Québec. What was often lacking, however, was the political will to enforce it. Even though it was the middle of summer, I gathered a team and we produced a plan to bring together all the environmental and agricultural groups in the area. We held a major news conference on the shores of Missisquoi Bay and got to work bringing everyone on side. The initiative was a huge success. The plan we applied produced an immediate measurable improvement. We were working to generalize its application throughout the province when I left the Cabinet. Unfortunately, the plan didn't proceed any further, and, as a result, many regions of Québec went through serious episodes of blue-green algae blooms in the summers of 2006 and 2007.

On November 25, 2004, I announced a sustainable development plan and tabled a draft Sustainable Development Act, amending the Québec Charter of Human Rights and Freedoms and affirming a new right to live in a healthy environment that respects biodiversity. The legislation that was later adopted unanimously by the *Assemblée nationale* was the most avant-garde initiative of its kind in North America. On December 15, the Cabinet approved modifying the regulations governing agriculture, and in particular hog farms, to conform to principles of sustainable development. The subsequent lifting of the moratorium on hog farm expansion in the province, while initially controversial, eventually satisfied the Union of Municipalities and citizens' groups, once the conditions placed on it were understood.

At first the powerful UPA (*Union des producteurs agricoles*), the Union of Agricultural Producers, had argued against the measures. Laurent Pellerin was its president, and his union represented every agricultural producer in the province of Québec. He had been on my short list of people who had to be met as soon as possible upon being sworn in as environment minister. A long-standing battle between the UPA and the previous Parti Québécois government had left many casualties, both political and economic, and it was a top priority for our new government to mend fences. Pellerin was himself a pork producer. Highly respected by his peers, he was an imposing figure with a thorough grasp of the issues under his purview. Whenever a minister had tried to take him on he had come out on top. Built like a fire hydrant, he was direct and confident, and he commanded respect. A minister in the previous government had railed against *"les barons du porc"* ("the pork barons"), an odd choice of words that sought to convey the disproportionate strength of several huge integrated pork producers and affiliated meat processing and packing operations. It became a rallying cry for producers, their "let them eat cake" moment, summarizing the insult they felt was being thrown at them by a government that didn't understand the tough realities of earning a living on the land. As the market had shifted, much of the top-quality pork for the lucrative Asian markets was now being produced in Québec, and the size and number of farms and production plants feeding the chain had grown exponentially. So, too, had the conflicts between neighbours, often the residents of small towns adjoining the hog farms.

The previous government had imposed a moratorium on new hog farms in the province, a measure that was fiercely opposed by the producers. Some farmers appeared to go out of their way to publicize their disapproval, for example, by deciding that the best time to spray pig manure on their fields was during the annual village festival. Social conflicts broke out across many rural areas, and each application for a new pig farm turned into a pitched battle, often with city-based environmental groups weighing in for good measure. It was a very tense situation. The PQ government's decision to impose a moratorium had earned it the bitter enmity of the UPA. It was against that backdrop that Mr. Pellerin and I had our first meeting in my office on the thirtieth floor of the major government building overlooking the *Assemblée nationale*.

The UPA president was wary at first, yet determined, as I was, to find a solution. We spoke at length, with very few staff present. It was to be the first of several meetings, in public and in private, and we hit it off very well. We both knew that the phosphorous load in some of the beautiful rivers of southern Québec had increased way beyond acceptable levels, causing major blue-green algae blooms and a proliferation of hypoxic or "dead" zones, oxygen-depleted areas that led to ecosystem die-offs. Local conflicts over odours and failure to contain slurry had to be addressed. Finally, I looked him in the eye and said something that would come to define our relationship: "Mr. Pellerin, 95 percent of your members respect every line of every article of every environmental and agricultural statute." He sat there, thought about that for a second, and countered: "Ninety-nine percent." I said, "Fair enough, 99 percent ... and that comes at a cost." There I also had no trouble getting agreement: compliance came at a cost. "So when someone doesn't respect the law, and it's not enforced, he's giving himself an economic advantage over his competitors, in addition to hurting the environment and the reputation of all producers." He again agreed. To drive my point home, I used a familiar sports analogy: "So instead of protecting and defending the 1 percent who *are* cheating, give me the number on their jerseys and I will start doing something that hasn't been done until now: enforcing the law and applying it equally to everyone."

We ended the meeting with a handshake and an agreement on two things. First, the rules would be clarified and made to reduce conflicts between neighbours. A concrete example was a series of restrictions on when and how manure could be spread. We simply agreed to go to an injection system, as opposed to spraying from the top. Second, rules would be enforced and applied equally to all. Tough issues would be discussed directly between him and me. Our handshake sealed an agreement that we both always respected: we would talk to each other and never use the type of hurtful language that had set off the battles with the previous government.

Containment turned out to be a tricky issue. If you were passing through a rural area where there was a lot of dairy production, as was the case in Québec, you noticed that there was always a large pile of manure on the field, at the end of a long conveyor leading from the barn. Containment had to become the norm, because a lot of the slurry was leaching into rivers and streams. The fight was over how to do it. Senior officials at the environment and agriculture ministries had been discussing and indeed arguing the issue of manure in fields for months. André Dicaire, the extremely effective *Secrétaire général du Conseil exécutif*, the equivalent of the Clerk of the Privy Council, who is the head of the civil service and deputy minister to the prime minister in Ottawa, had a strong background in agricultural matters and had been tasked directly with overseeing the discussions. While the matter may seem trifling, the costs to the average producer were anything but. Maintaining the peace and avoiding a return to the conflicts and moratoriums that had caused the crisis was a top priority for our government.

As a minister, watching battle lines being drawn between highly competent and determined senior civil servants can be a bit frustrating. The Ministry of Agriculture, Fisheries and Food appeared at times to be representing the producers and not the public. My own officials at Environment at times seemed to favour an approach that was great in theory but was in fact poorly adapted to the situation on the ground. I asked a simple question: "What's the result we are seeking?" The answer was equally simple: "No more leaching into streams and rivers, and protecting the groundwater." Fair enough, I said. Instead of proceeding, as officials at the ministry had been proposing, with an endless technical description of slopes, conditions, and requirements, I suggested that we go for an approach that described the result we required, as opposed to one that dictated the means. It worked.

The same results-oriented approach served me well when I had to deal with direct enforcement. We created a stand-alone enforcement agency that, together with other measures we introduced, allowed us to cut the ministry budgets during my three-year tenure while increasing inspections by 50 percent.

When we held committee hearings in the *Assemblée nationale*, I was again able to bring up my handshake deal with Laurent Pellerin, in more formal terms. He was appearing as a key witness, and I asked him what I was to do if one of the very negligible number of non-compliant producers persisted in breaking the law, despite all our attempts to obtain compliance. He reminded me that we had agreed on a working protocol, that both UPA and the department of the environment would always work together toward a solution but, at the end of the day, if a hog producer simply chose to continue ignoring the rules when everyone else was complying, then yes, tough enforcement measures were needed. That outcome — having our verbal agreement publicly reiterated in a very formal setting — was the result of fair dealing and working together to build trust on both sides. In the Beauce area south of Québec City there was a substantial hog farm whose owner had defied every entreaty from the UPA and every formal warning and attempt at enforcement from the ministry. As the minister responsible, it was up to me to act and to send a clear message. But on a personal and human level, it was one of the toughest decisions I'd ever taken. In mid-January 2006 about a dozen squad cars of the *Sûreté du Québec* along with large trailers and teams from our department drove onto the property, seized the herd, and put the producer out of business.

In 2008, after becoming a member of Parliament and NDP leader Jack Layton's Québec lieutenant, I was pleasantly surprised to receive an invitation to Laurent Pellerin's retirement party at the Auberge des Gouverneurs in Shawinigan. I knew it would be a long drive to get Jack there and I always tried to choose wisely when prevailing upon Jack to attend events, because I knew what his schedule was like. I explained how important Mr. Pellerin was and that there would be a lot of people there who'd love to see him. Jack's press secretary Karl Bélanger (today my principal secretary) was scheduled to accompany us, but Jack decided that we should just go without any of our aides. We set off for Shawinigan, and when Jack got there he was welcomed like a rock star. In our years of criss-crossing the province to build the Orange Wave, that night in Shawinigan stands out more than any other single event. It was a turning point, less for what occurred there than for what it revealed. There were hundreds of people there. Jack and I were treated extremely well. Everyone realized we'd travelled from Ottawa to be with them and they really appreciated it. More importantly, they knew Jack, they knew me, and they wanted to hear what we had to say. I was gobsmacked when Mr. Pellerin mentioned that he'd been following the work of our colleague in the NDP caucus, MP Alex Atamanenko, on food security. That he could actually discuss our position and knew Alex by name really impressed me, and it was very revealing. We had messages that were reaching people from every background and making their way into many different fields. The evening was an incredible success. That day both Jack and I realized something was happening for us in Québec.

Chapter Eleven
Storm Clouds

Rigorous enforcement, irrespective of the size of the business or the influence of the mayor, had been my approach as environment minister. It didn't sit well with some municipal authorities that had allowed precious wetlands in the Montréal area to be backfilled and developed despite rules that, on paper at least, were supposed to protect them.

On Montréal's South Shore, the largest city, Longueuil, was no exception. There, local environmental groups had been working hard to protect some of the wetlands that were home to protected species. I remember a very cordial meeting with the mayor, who had been complaining publicly that a lot of development was being held up because the Ministry of Sustainable Development, Environment and Parks was insisting on having a comprehensive plan to protect wetlands. He just saw no reason why the old way of doing things — paying lip service to the rules and developing anyway — shouldn't simply continue. At the time, wetlands could be bought for practically nothing. Developing them increased their value dramatically, so the charade always began with local officials and developers trying to get permission for their projects, and when that was refused, more often than not they just went ahead and developed the land. Any fine that the developers had to pay was no more than spare change compared to the greatly enhanced value of the property. I made it clear to the mayor of Longueuil that the times had changed and that only some of the projects would be allowed to proceed, on condition that we could agree on an overall plan to protect the wetlands. He accepted my offer, and the plan was prepared and approved. It was a win-win solution, both for the mayor and for the environment of Longueuil.

The biggest challenge came in Laval. From the beginning, the mayor of Laval, Gilles Vaillancourt, and my department were at loggerheads over the definition of what constituted a protected flood zone, as any enforcement of that definition would greatly restrict development in some areas of the island city. Predictably, the protection of these wetlands, which, coincidentally, were situated in my riding of Chomedey, also quickly became a flashpoint.

In 2005 we learned of an illegal development in western Laval, where a developer had gone ahead and developed a large tract of land including clearly protected areas. Instead of fining the developer after the fact, as the department had always done and which we knew would have little effect, I decided that it was time to send a strong signal that this was no longer how things would be done. I consulted our legal team. Did we have a more stringent approach available to us? Our lawyers said we did, but it had never been tried before: I could issue an order forcing the developer to restore the wetland to its original pristine state. So that's what we did. I issued the order in August 2005.

I had just completed a wide-ranging twenty-one-city tour of public consultations on my draft Sustainable Development Act, starting in Kuujjuaq on Ungava Bay in February and criss-crossing the province right into April, with Alain Gaul, my chief of staff, occasionally along to provide guidance, and Chantale Turgeon, my press secretary, as my wagon master. To oversee the whole operation, Alain had tapped Isabelle Perras, a very respected, experienced hand, whose wisdom and determination inspired the entire team. Everything was going well, and the legislation was ready to go, when a Cabinet meeting was called in August.

The order to restore the wetlands in Laval had just been issued and had received very favourable front page coverage, with a piece by Louis-Gilles Francœur, the highly respected environmental reporter for *Le Devoir*. He has since gone on to sit as vice-president of the *Bureau d'audiences publiques sur l'environnement* (BAPE), the independent public environmental review board charged with assessing development projects in the province.

It was the first time that Premier Charest and I had a disagreement, and it came as quite a surprise. He clearly wasn't pleased and told me so in no uncertain terms. I remember asking him if he was telling me that I should apply the rules one way in Longueuil and another in Laval. It was a bolt from the blue. After all, hadn't Charest himself been minister of the environment in the federal government? When I got back to the office I was still winded. I sat down with Alain and went over the day's events. I was going to stick to my guns.

From then on, in contrast to the first two and half years of my mandate, relations became frosty between the premier and me. There were several more disagreements, one of them over the Coca-Cola corporation. Since the 1980s Québec had had a law on the books on recycling soft drink cans that, to make things simpler, was also applied by the companies to juices. One day Coke decided that it was no longer going to charge the five-cent deposit on the juice cans, which meant that they could no longer be recycled as part of the deposit and return system. When François Cardinal, the environmental reporter for *La Presse* who has since joined the paper's editorial board, asked me what I was going to do about it, I said I wasn't going to allow it. That didn't sit well with the premier.

Our next serious disagreement came in the fall of 2005, over the Rabaska project — a methane and liquid natural gas plant and methane terminal that was being planned for the port of Lévis, across the St. Lawrence from Québec City, by a private consortium including Enbridge, Gaz Métro, and Gaz de France. Local environmental and citizens' groups vehemently opposed it.

In early 2006 I decided to go down to Boston and have a look at the Everett deliquification plant situated there. The plant was close to a bridge that was very reminiscent of the Jacques Cartier Bridge in Montréal. As with the proposal for Lévis, the liquid natural gas came into port in massive tankers. I met with U.S. officials, including the senior level of the U.S. Coast Guard, who turned out to be very helpful and truly exceptional people, to ask them how safe those installations were.

"You should see what we have to do every time a ship comes in," one of them replied. "We have to shut down the whole bridge. The plant is far too close to a civilian population. It's a huge mistake. We would never allow that gasification plant to be built so close to a large population today."

I described to them the Rabaska project that was being planned on the St. Lawrence, right across from Québec City, a metropolitan area numbering close to a million people. They warned that it was extremely dangerous and should never be allowed, which only confirmed my own and my department's evaluation. I went home to Québec more determined than ever to block the project.

While all this was going on, an even more contentious matter that had been simmering for a more than a year was about to come to a boil. Mont-Orford provincial park, established in 1938, covers nearly sixty square kilometres of lakes, rivers, mountains, and valleys, featuring great downhill and cross-country skiing. As the Mont-Orford ski hill was losing money and there were fears for its financial viability, the premier and several of his ministers had negotiated a deal to sell 649 hectares of parkland surrounding the ski hill to private developers. The provincial government was proposing to sell off a significant swath of public land that had been set aside in perpetuity for future generations. Mont-Orford was in the premier's electoral backyard. He went on record supporting the deal and made it clear he wanted the project approved as soon as possible. I was also under considerable pressure from colleagues who urged me to deliver for "the team." At the end of the day, though, I was being asked to sign a document selling off public land in a provincial park to private developers. We had a clear legal opinion that as long as the land could still be used for a park, selling it off was illegal. I simply couldn't do it. It was a matter of principle. I refused.

In politics we'd better stand for something, because we're often faced with decisions that force us to weigh private interests against the public interest. You need strong convictions. Conviction is what gives you strength to fight the battles that must be fought, to do the job the voters sent you to do, which is to faithfully convey, protect, and defend their interests. We are elected to represent them, to be their voice in our parliaments, in our governments, in Cabinet, as the case may be, and to influence government decisions on their behalf. They place their trust in us and we must never forget why they elect us.

On that score, the Frank Capra classic *Mr. Smith Goes to Washington,* released in 1939, is one of my favourite movies. At the time, it struck a chord with the audience because it exposed the cynicism of American politicians (senators, as it happens), their collusion with private interests, and the corrupting influence of money in the corridors of power. And it showed how even just one average citizen (the ineffable Jefferson Smith, played by James Stewart), an apparent country bumpkin who reveres Abraham Lincoln and believes every word of the American Constitution, manages to expose, denounce, and purge the whole rotten system simply by holding fast to his ideals and refusing to give up his principles. It's a movie that anyone interested in politics should see.

On Super Bowl Sunday, after I got back from my on-site consultations concerning the Everett deliquification plant in Boston, the proverbial manure finally hit the fan. I spoke to the premier on the phone and told him that going ahead with Rabaska would present a clear and obvious danger to the public, and that I wasn't going to submit it to the BAPE for impact assessment. Charest had publicly expressed his support for Rabaska, even though it had not been assessed by the BAPE. The conversation ended abruptly.

A few days later, as I was testifying on behalf of my department at the *Tribunal administratif du Québec,* Monsieur Julien, my bodyguard, received a call on his cell from the premier's office. As environment minister I had to spend a lot of time in court. When I'd begun my mandate, three years earlier, I'd been called to defend decisions taken by my predecessors, stretching back to my friend Pierre Paradis, when he was the minister, and to the PQ's Paul Bégin, with whom I'd crossed swords many times when he was minister of justice and I was Justice critic in the shadow Cabinet. I remember bumping into him after spending a day defending a measure he'd taken, and sharing a good laugh with him over it.

This kind of interaction is difficult to imagine for people outside the rarefied world of politics. Parliamentarians, much like lawyers, are normally able to put aside their briefs when they step outside the ring after pummelling each other all day long. I'll always remember the day in Québec City when the PQ called for my resignation in the *Assemblée nationale*. Quite a feat, considering that I was still in the Opposition at the time! I don't recall what *crime de lèse-majesté* I had committed to get under the PQ government's skin that particular day, but when François Gendron, then a highly experienced PQ Cabinet minister, and I met up on our way out of the Chamber next to the door that is used mainly by MNAs and journalists, we started kibbitzing and he jokingly grabbed me by the collar, calling me *"mon moineau"* (a jocular term of endearment that literally translates as "my sparrow" and is roughly equivalent to "You character!"). A seasoned journalist who happened to be walking by stopped in his tracks. "Wait a minute," he asked Gendron, "didn't your side just call for Mulcair's resignation?" *"Ben, voyons donc,"* ("Oh, come off it,") my PQ colleague intoned. "That kind of thing happens in there. When we're out here, we move on." François is now the dean of the *Assemblée nationale*. His ability to distinguish between political skirmishing and real life is one of the reasons for his longevity.

Another political adversary who, for the same reasons, was a friend in "real life" was the late Jim Flaherty. We both had the Irish, as they say, had both grown up around Montréal, both played hockey (occasionally on opposite teams, as in that memorable game in Maple Leaf Gardens), and shared the same brand of Irish humour. His sudden and untimely death in April 2014 affected all those who knew him very personally, no matter which party we belonged to.

The reason I was in court that morning in February 2006 was that I had issued an order stopping a quarrying operation on the magnificent north slope of the St. Lawrence, east of Québec City. The project had been highly controversial locally but would likely have gone through were it not for a couple of nearby residences that had been overlooked, which was how we'd been able to put a halt to the project. As soon as I finished, Monsieur Julien informed me that the premier wanted to see me in his office.

When my press secretary Chantale Turgeon and I got there, she sat down to wait in the anteroom and I went into the premier's office. Mr. Charest made his intentions clear immediately. I was being moved out of Environment and offered another portfolio that was basically an empty shell. Of course my discretion was expected on the whole matter.

Though I already knew my answer and that Catherine would support it, I requested a time out to talk with my family. I went into an adjoining room and got hold of Catherine. She was busy with patients but had told the receptionist to come and get her if I called, because we'd known for some time that the writing was on the wall. "I'm just going to quit," I said. "I'm throwing back the keys to the limo. But I'm going to stick around. I'll finish my mandate. I'll fulfill my commitment to my constituents. But I'm not going to make this decision alone. What do you think?"

Catherine backed me all the way. After I hung up I managed to get hold of Matt, who by then had been a police officer for several years, and was also able to track down Greg at the firm where he was now working as an aerospace engineer. The decision was unanimous, from all four of us, together. I went back into the premier's office and told him I wasn't going to take his offer. I was going to leave the Cabinet and serve out my mandate as the member of the *Assemblée nationale* for Chomedey. Charest looked taken aback. He hadn't expected that someone who was already in Cabinet could give up the perks and privileges that went with the title.

When I came out of his office, Chantale was still waiting in an adjoining room. I had been with the premier for an unusually long time. She looked at me and, without an inkling of what had just happened, said to me, "You look relieved." "Indeed I am," I said. "Indeed I am." At the very first Cabinet meeting after I resigned, my successor had the sale of Mont-Orford land approved. Charest finally had his order-in-council.

As for me, I'd left with a clear conscience and I was proud of the work done by everyone in my department during my term as minister of sustainable development, environment and parks during those three years. I've always understood that those of us who hold public office have a responsibility to get results for people, while managing the public purse with the utmost rigour. That was the approach I took when I was named to the provincial Cabinet. I oversaw a reduction by almost 10 percent of the province's greenhouse gas emissions, the best result among Canada's largest provinces, and by creating a stand-alone enforcement agency we were also able to increase inspections by 50 percent while simultaneously reducing our departmental budget year over year.

I went on sitting in the *Assemblée nationale* on behalf of my constituents. When there were public hearings, and the developer who'd set his sights on Mont-Orford was called in to testify, I was there, bearing witness to the proceedings. Two months later, in April 2006, I got to vote on the Sustainable Development Act I'd fought so hard to put in place and see it adopted unanimously by my colleagues in the *Assemblée nationale*. Claude Béchard had replaced me at Environment. That same year, faced with the mounting public backlash over the whole Mont-Orford controversy, he was forced to cancel the planned development, and to appease the fury of citizens' groups in the area he ended up doubling the size of Mont-Orford provincial park. The following year, in 2007, Béchard's successor, Line Beauchamp, announced that no development would be permitted in Mont-Orford park, period.

Chapter Twelve
A New Beginning

While I served out my mandate as MNA for Chomedey, Pierre Paradis, who by then was *persona non grata* because he was too much of a free spirit, and I used to sit together in our assigned seats at the far end of the government side of the Chamber and joke about our situation. But the fact remained that my resignation did not sit well with my former colleagues, and there was a fair bit of acrimony and hard feelings.

As I was no longer a member of Cabinet, I had to give up most of the spacious office space I had been using. My staff and I proceeded to move the riding into much smaller premises. From then on, I shared the office with Chantale Turgeon, my press secretary, while Graham Carpenter, my riding assistant, had to camp out in the kitchen.

That spring of 2006 I began getting calls from the federal parties in Ottawa. The very first call I got was from an anglophone Green Party member living in Lévis, a very articulate guy who urged me to join the Greens. For me, that wasn't a realistic option. I honestly shared Québec environmentalist Steven Guilbeault's analysis when he said that the best way to make sure that nothing gets done on the environment is to marginalize it by voting for a single-issue party.

The next call, at the end of May or early June, came in to Graham Carpenter at the riding office. The call was from Pierre Ducasse, who at the time was Québec adviser in Jack Layton's office and one of the New Democratic Party's longest serving organizers in the province. He was calling for and on behalf of his leader, and I agreed to speak with Mr. Layton by phone. We had a pleasant conversation and further agreed that we should get together at some point. Later that summer I got another call from a friend named Brian MacInnis whom I had worked with at Alliance Québec and who was good friends with Jack and Olivia. That was Jack's way, and it was brilliant. Jack didn't recruit candidates. He took great care to court them. Unbeknownst to me, he was asking everybody he knew who had ever known me to call me and say I should consider running for the NDP. I was flattered by the attention, but didn't think more of it than that. Jack was determined, however, and we spoke again later on in the summer.

Meanwhile, the Conservatives also came calling. A senior Conservative who was an old friend from Québec City, tried very hard to recruit me. As an environmentalist, I had been interested in chairing the National Round Table on the Environment and the Economy (NRTEE), an independent policy advisory agency of the government of Canada. It had been created in 1988 by the Mulroney government in the wake of the famous 1987 Brundtland report, *Our Common Future,* on the environment and the need for sustainable economic development. The NRTEE brought together hundreds of experts, business and community leaders from across Canada with first-hand knowledge in a variety of areas. I had put forward my name, and had been short-listed to head the agency. The Conservatives worked hard to get me on board, but it was clear from my last conversation with them that they had no intention of doing anything constructive on the environment, which has since been borne out by the facts. As I had also had a serious offer from a top-tier law firm to work in its environmental section, Catherine and I talked one more time. "Ask yourself," she said, as only she knows how. "Are you truly certain that your political career is over? Or is there a chance that you might want to run again?" I came to the conclusion that I couldn't rule it out completely and we both agreed that if I was going to make a return to politics, it was going to be with Jack Layton and the NDP, which so closely mirrored all of our deepest values and convictions.

When Jack had won the leadership of the NDP in 2003, he said he wanted to make Québec a priority. At the time many in the party just rolled their eyes, because they had talked for years about the importance of Québec for the NDP without ever having anything to show for it. But for Jack these weren't empty words. Jack had been born in Québec, he had grown up there, and he was quite sensitive to the issues Québecers cared about. His commitment to finally achieve a breakthrough for the NDP in the province was utterly sincere.

Fast-forward three years to September 9, 2006, right after Labour Day, when the NDP held its national convention in Québec City, its first in the province. It was a daring move that spoke to Jack's decision back in 2003 to make Québec a priority. When we had spoken the second time, I'd suggested that he invite me to come to the convention and give a speech on my signature legislation on sustainable development. He thought that was a great idea, so on the Saturday of the convention I went up to Québec City, as agreed. The Québec media were out in force. The convention was a big deal, and the news that I planned to give a speech had made the front page of *Le Soleil,* along with a big colour photo of me, under the headline *"Mulcair parlera au NPD"* ("Mulcair to speak to the NDP").

When it came to Québec, as in so many things, Jack was a truly far-sighted leader. Jack meant business. In 2004 Jack assigned a group led by Pierre Ducasse to draft a document that would very clearly state where we stood regarding Québec's place in Canada. Over the next three years, Pierre, in consultation with Jack and prominent Québecers like Nycole Turmel and Charles Taylor, who had served on the committee on the future of social democracy in Canada commissioned by then party leader Alexa McDonough, worked on drafting a document that was submitted for adoption at the general council meeting of the NDP Québec section. The meeting took place in Sherbrooke in May 2005, and the document became known as the Sherbrooke Declaration. It recognized Québec's national character and promoted a vision of asymmetrical federalism based on the fact that Québecois culture and institutions have evolved differently than those in the rest of the country. When Jack had sent it to me to read, I'd been impressed by its positive, upbeat vision of what could be done to make a place for Québec in Canada that Québecers would embrace. The declaration adopted in Sherbrooke in 2005 was about to be ratified at that 2006 NDP convention in Québec City to which I had been invited.

After my speech that day many people approached me to say how glad they were to see me there. I met delegates from every part of Québec, some of whom had been active in the NDP for years. The convention attracted a lot of notice. Later that winter, I learned from Diana Bronson, who was a member of the NDP leader's staff, that Jack would be coming to Montréal to give a speech on the Afghan War at the Université de Montréal. I decided to attend. His speech, stating that the Afghanistan adventure had gone on long enough, that it had been far too costly in lives and treasure, and that it was time for a concerted effort for peace and to bring the troops home, was very well received.

Afterward, Jack and I went out to lunch. That was when I learned that he had some very capable people working for him. Karl Bélanger, his senior press secretary (who is now my principal secretary as leader of the Official Opposition in Ottawa) was with us, and he really impressed me. When we got out of the car at the restaurant, lo and behold, waiting to snap our picture was a photographer from the Canadian Press who turned out to be none other than Robert Galbraith — the man Catherine and I had met during his hunger strike in the summer of 2003. That night and the following morning, the photo he took of Jack and me was all over the media, along with the news that I was clearly talking to the NDP.

That November Catherine and I had an unforgettable supper with Jack and Olivia in Hudson, Québec, the place where Jack grew up. We met at Mon Village restaurant and spent a lovely evening together. During that dinner, Catherine, who is a listener and not very easy to persuade, was thoroughly smitten with Jack's vision for Canada and Canadians. Jack was also an excellent strategist and tactician. As he and I discussed the political challenges he and his party faced, Jack looked at me and said something I'll never forget. "In the next campaign, I'm going to announce that I'm running for prime minister," he opened. I must have looked unimpressed. "No, no, bear with me," he continued. "Just *saying that* is actually going to be revolutionary, because no leader of the NDP has ever gone before the cameras to declare they were running for the job of prime minister of Canada. So it's going to be a bit of a sea change, even for our own people. I know that Canadians might look at me and raise an eyebrow, thinking 'Come on, that's not going to happen.' I get that, because I understand one thing, which is that we can't hope to form a government unless we first become the Official Opposition. That's as clear to me as 2 + 2 = 4. We can talk all we want about forming the government, but we'll never get to be a contender unless we form the Official Opposition first and show ourselves capable of doing that job. And we can't hope to form the Official Opposition unless we win a significant number of seats in Québec." Then he paused and added, "That's where you come in." The NDP had done some polling in the federal riding of Outremont, where a by-election was going to be held later that year. When people in the sample were asked which party was their second choice, two-thirds of Bloc voters answered it was the NDP.

I gathered together my family council — Catherine, Greg, Matt and Jasmyne, and a couple of dear family friends — just as I had when I'd stepped down as environment minister. Everyone I knew professionally thought a run for the NDP was career suicide; my family had a very different take. In the end, my sons Matt and Greg put it most succinctly: "You believe in this man," they said. "You believe he's got a shot at a breakthrough in Québec, and the NDP is clearly the party that shares your values. After everything you just went through, having to resign a job you loved as environment minister, shouldn't you listen to that?" Here I was, fifty-two years old, at a crossroads in my career, and my children were telling me to take a chance and follow my heart. No father could ask for better kids.

A few months later Jack introduced me to Rebecca Blaikie, the daughter of former NDP MP Bill Blaikie. Rebecca was our party organizer in Québec. Jack hadn't told his Québec organizers who the mystery "star candidate" was that he'd asked them to come and meet, after hours, at the federal office in Ottawa, but, as Rebecca told me later, she, Raoul Gébert, and Nicholas Dominic, two of the fine young people working on the ground for us in Québec, were sure it was going to be me. (Romeo Saganash and I had apparently been on their "dream list" of candidates for at least a year. Romeo is now our NDP MP for Abitibi–Baie-James–Nunavik–Eeyou.) After the meeting Rebecca rushed back to Montréal to plan the press conference at which we were going to announce I'd be ooolting to run for the NDP.

On April 20, 2007, Jack and I met the media at Smith House, on Mount Royal, to make the announcement and say that I would be acting as Jack's Québec lieutenant. After I made the change from provincial to federal politics, I was often asked by journalists why I'd switched parties. The answer is really not all that complicated. In Québec, the parties were not so much defined by social or economic issues as artificially divided on much more abstract but deeply emotional constitutional lines regarding Québec's relationship with Canada. The Québec Liberal Party and the Parti Québécois were two "big tents," with federalists flocking to the Québec Liberal Party and sovereignists to the PQ. But on social and economic issues, both congregations ran the gamut from right-wing conservatives to left-wing progressives. In contrast, on the federal level, voters in Québec and across Canada have a clear progressive choice: the NDP.

Québec's unique political paradigm had emerged in the 1960s, when René Lévesque, who had been one the most progressive ministers in the government of Québec Premier Jean Lesage until the Liberals lost the election in 1966, left the party to promote the idea of a sovereign Québec in economic association with Canada. Within a year, Lévesque had helped found the Parti Québécois, drawing together two other separatist parties and attracting Liberals and right-wing Union Nationale supporters for whom Québec's constitutional status trumped all other issues.

Under Lévesque's charismatic leadership and with the support of labour and other progressive activists who joined in droves, the new sovereignist party crafted a platform that was very progressive on socio-economic issues. Many Québecers who weren't in favour of separation but held progressive views began voting for the PQ. From then on the Liberals became identified as the party that opposed Québec separation, and Québecers whose attachment to Canada trumped their views on all other issues became the Liberal Party base. This also created a strange new landscape in which Jean Charest, the leader of the federal Conservatives, could be drafted to lead the provincial Liberal Party and later preside over a Cabinet that included Henri-François Gautrin, who'd spoken at my first NDP meeting in 1974 and whose progressive convictions, two decades later, were still rock-solid.

Québec has had a strong progressive tradition going back to the nineteenth century, though it is too often obscured by memories of the *Grande*

Noirceur ("great darkness") of the Duplessis era that began in the late 1930s and stretched on until the dawn of the Quiet Revolution in the early 1960s. Much has been written about Premier Jean Lesage's ground-breaking reforms: full nationalization of electricity under the then Liberal minister of natural resources, René Lévesque; the end of church domination over schools and hospitals; the creation practically overnight of a complete system of public education with, for the first time, a Department of Education headed by a senior Cabinet minister. But there had also been an earlier progressive interval between the first and second Duplessis regimes under Liberal Premier Adélard Godbout. Sadly, it has practically vanished from public memory.

Godbout was in office for just one term, from 1939 to 1944, yet in that short time he managed to bring in reforms that foreshadowed the Quiet Revolution. He instituted women's suffrage in 1940; free primary education and compulsory school attendance for all children up to the age of fourteen; a public service commission; a Labour Code affirming the right of workers to form unions and to negotiate collective agreements; and the beginnings of a public utility grid, creating Hydro-Québec into the bargain. One can only imagine what his government could have accomplished had it been re-elected. Montréal historian Frank Guttman has authored a fascinating book on one of Godbout's key ministers, Télesphore-Damien Bouchard. Guttman's book, *The Devil from Saint-Hyacinthe,* after an epithet thrown at T.-D. Bouchard by Duplessis himself, is a splendid account of Bouchard's role as leader of the Opposition in the *Assemblée nationale* from 1936 to 1939, when he fought against the first Duplessis government's authoritarian policies.

Whereas for most of the twentieth century, progressives were generally found on the *Rouge* side of the aisle, after René Lévesque left the Liberal Party to found the PQ many progressives followed him. With the coming of the PQ, Québec independence became the dominant political issue dividing the electorate. Suddenly, progressives who were deeply attached to their Canadian identity found themselves fighting with other progressives in the sovereignist camp. But when the members of the *Assemblée nationale* undertake to craft legislation on big social policy issues like publicly funded, affordable child care, it's fascinating to watch party lines become blurred and a consensus emerge that in any other Canadian province would be called progressive, or downright social democratic.

That's part of the upside of the otherwise frustrating absence at the ballot box of a clearly defined social democratic option. Up until the last two election cycles, when the PQ's rightward drift led many progressives to leave the fold and join or found newer, smaller parties, progressives on either side of the constitutional divide often made common cause on sometimes thorny social issues. They still do. The best recent example was the sterling work that was accomplished on end-of-life medical care (or "dying with dignity," as the legislation is called in French), when the government struck a special committee responsible for holding province-wide public consultations. It was co-chaired by two extraordinary progressives: Geoff Kelley from the Québec Liberal Party and Véronique Hivon from the PQ. The resulting Bill 52 was tabled in the *Assemblée nationale* by then PQ minister Hivon and became law under the Liberal government of Philippe Couillard, who allowed his MNAs to vote their conscience. Only twenty-two of his MNAs opposed it, and Québec became the first Canadian province to legalize doctor-assisted end-of-life care.

In Québec the artificial dividing line between the two camps had begun to break down as early as 1989. That year, Mario Dumont, who was the president of the Québec Liberal Party's youth wing and a strong nationalist, broke away from the QLP on constitutional grounds and founded his own right-of-centre party, the Action démocratique du Québec (ADQ). In the 1995 referendum Dumont was to side with the pro-sovereignty "Yes" camp, but thereafter he steered his party away from taking a sharply defined constitutional stand and concentrated on promoting a right-wing economic agenda. Lucien Bouchard himself, after doing so much to help lift the "Yes" side to within a hair's breadth of victory in 1995, refused to hold a third referendum and governed like a conservative during his tenure as premier. Under Bouchard's leadership the progressive base of the party chafed under "zero deficit" policies. Unwilling to put up with the growing dissent, Bouchard quit as premier in 2001. Five years later progressives who had been drifting away from the PQ founded their own party, Québec solidaire (QS). In 2008, co-founder Amir Khadir was elected to the *Assemblée nationale*, and again in 2012, this time along with party co-president Françoise David, a prominent figure in the women's equality and social justice movements. In April 2014 a third member, Manon Massé, another strong progressive, was added. As for the Parti Québécois, after drifting steadily rightward for a decade it briefly replaced the scandal-ridden Liberals, winning a bare minority in 2012, only to suffer a humiliating defeat less than two years later to the Québec Liberal Party under its new leader, Philippe Couillard.

One of the more intriguing recent arrivals on the Québec provincial political scene is Pierre Karl Péladeau, the member of the *Assemblée nationale* for the riding of Saint-Jérôme who, even though he is now the leader of the Parti Québécois, is still the primary shareholder of the Quebecor media empire.

During his tenure as CEO, "PKP," as he is known, imposed a record-breaking sixteen employee lockouts. During the lockout at the Quebecor-owned *Journal de Québec,* Jack and I spent a morning with the locked-out employees on a street corner, handing out copies of the newspaper they were publishing themselves. I'll never forget another visit Jack and I made to locked-out employees of the *Journal de Montréal,* also owned by Quebecor. Jack was holding a woman in his arms as she wept, recalling how she and her colleagues had built up the paper, going back to the days of its beloved founder, Pierre Karl Péladeau's father, and had given it value through decades of tireless work. The locked-out employees went on to found their own newspaper. Many of them volunteered for us during the lead-up to the Orange Wave and since 2011 have become active members of the NDP, because our party reflects their values.

In April 2007, after Jack named me his Québec lieutenant, he said he would ask his MPs if they would allow me to attend caucus and take part in our meetings. The NDP considers that anyone who's ever been elected federally under the party banner is welcome to attend the weekly caucus meetings when Parliament is sitting. Often when NDP stalwarts from past Parliaments show up for events in Ottawa, they take their place in the caucus room and are warmly welcomed by all. At the same time, the NDP has a hard and fast rule against floor crossing. Any MPs who leave their party and wish to join the NDP caucus must first resign and run in a by-election, or finish their mandate as independents and get elected under the NDP banner in the following election. When the impressive MP for the Montréal riding of Ahuntsic, Maria Mourani, was kicked out of the Bloc Québécois after the leader tried to muzzle her for opposing the PQ's discriminatory *Charte des valeurs québécoises* (Québec Charter of Values), she asked to join the NDP. We welcomed her membership but explained that she could not join the NDP caucus until she was re-elected under our banner by her constituents. She chose to sit alone as an independent until the next election and has now been chosen by party members in the riding of Ahuntsic as the NDP candidate in the riding.

For Jack to invite me into the caucus was therefore a huge honour, and the welcome I got from his MPs spoke volumes about their determination to grow the party in Québec. The very first meeting I attended dealt with the long-gun registry, a contentious issue that divided the country and posed a challenge to Jack, as it later did to me when I succeeded him as leader. The December 6, 1989, massacre of fourteen young women at the École Polytechnique (the Engineering Faculty of the Université de Montréal) by a deranged, hate-filled young man armed with a legally obtained military-style semi-automatic assault rifle, left the entire province traumatized and pushed the issue of gun control to the front of the political agenda. Because of the massacre at the Polytechnique and the 2006 shooting at Dawson College, most Québecers support the idea of having people register their guns. But the national gun registry issue had been badly mishandled by the federal Liberals, who had used criminal sanctions for even the most trifling errors and let the cost of the program balloon out of control. That allowed the policy to become the target of a well-orchestrated campaign by a pro-gun advocacy group with ties to the National Rifle Association (NRA), the powerful American gun lobby. Anger against the registry was compounded by the sense that rural Canadians were being unfairly made to pay the price for violence in the cities by politicians who had no understanding or respect for their way of life. At first, as a newcomer, I seriously underestimated the challenge of uniting people on this issue, along with Stephen Harper's talent for using a divisive issue as a political weapon against his opponents and the Liberals' willingness to play his game.

By the middle of May 2007, about six weeks after we announced that I had joined the NDP, it became clear that a by-election was about to be called in the federal riding of Outremont. The time had come to declare my candidacy. The day before we planned to announce, Bill Nash, a friend from high school, contacted me, not knowing that I was on the verge of going public, and said he'd been asked by a couple of very senior Liberals, whom he knew from his time on the board of the *Société de l'assurance automobile du Québec* (SAAQ), to deliver a very specific message. I could have any safe Liberal seat I wanted, they said, as long as I didn't declare for the NDP in any riding in Québec. I replied, "Tell them that they're going to get their answer tomorrow."

Even way back in 1968, when Robert Cliche, a highly respected Québec lawyer and Second World War veteran who later went on to become chief justice of the Québec Provincial Court, announced he was running for the NDP in the Montréal-area riding of Duvernay, the Liberals, who were in power in Ottawa, immediately asked Eric Kierans, who at the time was a minister in the Québec provincial government, to run against him. The same thing had happened to Charles Taylor in 1965, when he announced his candidacy for the NDP in Mount Royal, and they chose Pierre Trudeau to be their candidate. Even though our party had very little visibility in Québec, whenever we ran a high-profile candidate who had a reasonable chance of winning, whether it was Robert Cliche in 1963 and 1968, Charles Taylor in 1962, 1963, 1965, and 1968, or consumer advocate Phil Edmonston in 1988 and 1990 (the second time was in a by-election in Chambly, which he won, becoming the first NDP MP elected from Québec in Canadian history), the Liberals fought us tooth and nail. They obviously knew what an NDP breakthrough in Québec could mean.

Here it's important to remember what the NDP is: a social democratic party that came into being in 1961 out of the merger of the Co-operative Commonwealth Federation (CCF) and the Canadian Labour Congress. The CCF was born on the Prairies in the 1930s at the time of the Great Depression to alleviate the suffering of workers and farmers, of the ill and the old, of all those who had been driven to destitution in the aftermath of the catastrophic collapse of the financial system on Wall Street in 1929. Someone had to do it, because for the first few years after the crash, governments responded by wrong-headedly slashing spending, which only made a bad situation incomparably worse.

It's easy to forget that not so long ago in Canada there were no social programs, no safety net — no old age pensions, guaranteed income supplement, medicare, or unemployment insurance. If you were poor, and your child or someone you loved got ill, you either found a doctor who was willing to treat them for free or they got sicker until, in many cases, they died. If you were a farmer during the epic drought that desiccated the Prairies in those years, the banks repossessed your farm and sold your home, your animals, and every piece of equipment and stick of furniture you owned at auction. If you'd lost your job when the stock market crashed in 1929 and had remained jobless ever since, you rode the rails looking for work, knocked on people's back doors begging a bit of food, or ended up in one of the hobo jungles that had sprung up on the outskirts of major Canadian cities along the railway. Meanwhile, the lucky few wealthy enough to have survived the crash with their fortunes relatively intact saw their standard of living actually increase during the Depression, because the price of everything had hit rock bottom.

As for the Canadian Labour Congress, it's worth remembering that before right-wing parties in many Western countries, going back to the days of Ronald Reagan and Margaret Thatcher, began successfully attacking unions, the labour movement had been responsible for the greatest reduction in social inequality in history. It was unionized workers who forced governments to introduce the weekend (now eroded for many middle-class working families); the eight-hour day; the minimum wage; workers' compensation, without which, not so long ago, a work-related accident could mean financial disaster for an entire family; sick days; vacation days; … and the list goes on. In the past thirty years, the conservative and "centrist" governments that alternated in power in the developed world have torn progressively larger holes in the social safety net created in the wake of the Depression, claiming that our societies couldn't afford to keep it in good repair.

And yet, if you take a longer view, you can clearly see that the most prolonged, uninterrupted stretch of economic prosperity in history, the "golden decades," coincided with the period after the Second World War when wages were highest, and the strength and reach of social programs were at their peak. War-torn Europe had been rebuilt thanks to the Marshall

Plan, a massive infusion of public money that allowed the creation of millions of well-paying jobs and laid the foundations of the economic powerhouse that Germany became.

The social programs Canadians have come to rely on as a necessary part of maintaining their standard of living came out of policy ideas put forward by the CCF and the NDP, some of which, including our publicly funded, universal health-care system, were first introduced by NDP governments in the provinces. For a very long time these programs were politically untouchable. Not anymore. But during campaigns lip-service must be paid, because voters would not take kindly to knowing that the unemployment insurance and public pension plans that they've paid into all their lives won't be there if they find themselves out of a job or reach the age of sixty-five. The Liberals in particular have made a fine art of "flashing left and turning right," making progressive promises before elections only to shelve them once in power. Their national child-care program, promised in every election since 1993, is only the most flagrant example.

Ever since the PQ, almost overnight, became the alternative to the Québec Liberals, many nationalist voters who didn't necessarily agree with its separatist goal began "taking out insurance" at the federal level. This, as we've seen, was starkly evident during the early years, when Québecers voted en masse for René Lévesque's PQ at the provincial level and gave Pierre Trudeau's Liberals the majority of Québec seats in the House of Commons. Because Québec continued to be a wasteland for the Progressive Conservatives, going back to the days of Louis Riel, the Liberals were able to brand themselves as the party of national unity for nearly forty years, despite Brian Mulroney's attempt at repairing the broken china left by the Liberals' mishandled patriation of the Constitution.

But think about it. How shameless is it for any party to claim to be the sole guarantor of national unity or the sole protector of the nation's security? Pierre Trudeau's anti-separatist rhetoric angered a lot of moderate nationalist Québecers. The unilateral patriation of the Constitution, using strong-arm tactics denounced by both sovereignists and senior provincial Liberals, still remains a bitter memory for many in the province. Unsurprisingly, federal Liberals call this historical fact a myth, turning their backs on the necessary healing and reconciliation that has to happen in this generation of Canadians. Sadder still, the art of wedge politics perfected by the Liberals over the past four decades has worked so well that Stephen Harper has made it his stock in trade. Leaving aside national unity, an issue on which he's spent little time building any kind of credibility, this prime minister seeks to divide us on matters like war — any war — and national security. The aim that both of the old parties pursue when they resort to this tactic is to tar their opponents as unpatriotic, weak, unfit to protect Canadians.

We all love our country and our province, but whenever politicians wrap themselves in the flag in an attempt to scare up votes, it's wise to remember the words of the great British moralist Samuel Johnson, when he said, "Patriotism is the last refuge of a scoundrel."

In 2011, for the first time in a generation, Québecers voted for a federalist party in a federal election. Rather than bet on fear and division, the NDP appealed to Québecers' hearts and to the values they share with all Canadians. We were proposing an optimistic vision that could create "winning conditions" for Québec in Canada and for Canada in Québec.

Chapter Thirteen
Betting Against the Odds

One of the things I had to get used to right off the bat was the differ-ence in culture between the New Democratic Party of Canada and the Québec Liberal Party. The NDP is a movement as well as a party. It is extremely democratic and grassroots oriented, whereas the political culture I'd come from was entirely top-down and hierarchical. Right from the start I teased Rebecca Blaikie that she was my "interpreter" as I learned the ropes in my new political family. When I first joined the team, she and her colleagues worked out of a tiny apartment on Saint-Laurent Boulevard in Montréal. I used to call them *"les colocs"* for a laugh (the word *coloc* is Québec slang for "roommate," and Les Colocs had been a very popular Québec band in the 1990s). One of the first people Rebecca introduced me to was Steve Moran, a brilliant young linguist who spoke Chinese and Urdu as well as French fluently. In addition to his exceptional insight into how linguistic differences influence culture, he'd worked for NDP MP Svend Robinson for several years and, despite his young age, had acquired a deep knowledge of NDP culture and party history. Later, once I'd been elected, he was the first person I hired to run my parliamentary office in Ottawa. Like all the other NDP staff members I met, he was a true progressive. It was a great feeling to recognize my own principles and values in those of my party.

Finally the by-election was called for September 17, 2007, and we hit the ground running. Catherine and I had gone up to the cottage to recuperate from all the excitement of our son Matt's wedding, which had taken place on July 14. On July 28, a Saturday, my press secretary Chantale Turgeon reached me at the cottage and told me that the by-election had just been called. At noon, when I met her on the esplanade in front of *Maison Radio-Canada,* she had lined up an entire five-hour block of interviews with every radio station, TV station, and newspaper on the island of Montréal. When I asked her where the Liberal and Conservative candidates were going to be, she told me that both had informed the media that they would only be available for interviews the following week. We, on the other hand, were prepared to fight for every column inch and every second of air time. The upshot was that our full-court press produced great coverage for us over the next two days and even into Monday. As for our opponents, by the time they showed up the election call was no longer headline news.

When Jack had asked me to run for the NDP, he had promised me that the party would pour every resource it had into winning. Although Outremont is mostly French speaking and includes one of the most high-income franco-phone neighbourhoods in the province, it is also one of the most ethnically, religiously, and linguistically diverse ridings in the country, with very large Filipino, Hassidic, and francophone African communities. The availability of relatively low-rent housing has meant that the Côte-des-Neiges area of the riding was often the first place new Canadians settled when they arrived in Québec. About a hundred different mother tongues are spoken in the riding.

During the campaign, MPs from outside the province began coming in to lend us a hand. I can remember Niki Ashton arriving from Churchill, Manitoba, where she was an NDP volunteer. Her dad had been Manitoba environment minister as the same time as I had that job in Québec. We'd gone to Washington and worked together on the contentious issue of Devil's Lake. Niki spoke Greek in addition to French and English, and she was a huge hit with the Greek com-munity in Park Extension, a multi-ethnic neighbourhood that reached into the riding. They invited her back over and over again. Today she is a second-term colleague in our caucus and Official Opposition critic for Aboriginal affairs.

Jack's wife Olivia Chow was a dynamo and went door to door with me in the Chinese community. She also did wonderful work with the Vietnamese and Filipino communities, where I had made strong contacts when I headed the English-speaking Catholic Council. We worked non-stop, and it wasn't long before we could feel that something was happening.

I particularly remember one sunny Sunday afternoon in late August, toward the middle of the campaign. Rebecca and the team had organized a barbecue on the corner of Jeanne Mance Park, across Park Avenue from Mount Royal. Jack and Olivia had joined us, along with Ed Broadbent and Alexa McDonough, and people streamed in off the street to meet us all afternoon. At one point we had close to a hundred people, and I made a speech in which I declared: "An Orange Wave is coming, and it is going to sweep the province." Of course a lot of people smiled incredulously, but Rebecca caught my eye and nodded approvingly, because by then it was obvious to the campaigners on the ground that, in Outremont at least, we had a real shot at winning.

Right after I'd announced in April, Jack and I had gone on a tour of the province. Jack had a wish list with the names of the people whom he hoped were going to be running as NDP candidates in Québec in the next general election. These included the well-known Cree lawyer Romeo Saganash and the Montréal civil rights lawyer Julius Grey. One of the first stops on our tour was Québec City, where we had supper with Romeo. During the meal he told us the story of his brother, who'd been taken away to residential school at the age of six and never returned the following summer. Romeo's mother had spent years trying to find out what had happened to him and the better part of a lifetime locating where he was buried. As he described his mother's pain he got very emotional. Jack and I were moved to tears.

We next went up to the Saguenay, where Peter Julian, one of our MPs from British Columbia who is today our House Leader, had spent years working with people whose jobs were with forestry and mining companies, many of which were foreign owned and very hostile to unions. We made community visits and met Éric Dubois, with a very capable organizer who was working on recruiting a couple of local business people to run for us. After that we came back via Trois-Rivières and visited the Hydrogen Research Institute at the Université du Québec à Trois-Rivières (UQTR). What was interesting was that, at every stop along the way, whenever we made ourselves available to the media there would be a big pick-up. In Trois-Rivières there must have been six cameras at our little press conference. Clearly, out in the francophone heartland of the province, people were interested in Jack and curious about the NDP.

As election day approached, with only twelve days of campaigning left to go, we'd identified just two thousand supporters. Our accomplishment over the first five weeks of the campaign had been to convince voters not to lock in their vote in favour of another party — to give the NDP a serious look. But with voters tuned out from politics in the sunny months of July and August, they weren't quite ready to make up their minds for us, either. As Labour Day rolled around, with by-election day now just around the corner, people in the riding started talking to their neighbours, their family, their co-workers about the upcoming election — and, funny thing, they were mostly saying the same things. "The NDP has been out in force in this election." "I've received three phone calls from the NDP, a volunteer on my doorstep, and two pieces of mail." "I got a phone message from the NDP, but it wasn't to tell me to vote for them; it was to invite me to an event in my neighbourhood." "The Liberals seem to be taking the riding for granted." "I drove past the Liberal campaign office and there was nobody there at 5:00 p.m."

In Québec, political "lawn signs" go on public property, but rarely, if ever, on people's actual lawns. In a province where divisive national unity issues have dominated politics for so long, no one wants to provoke an unnecessary fight with their otherwise amiable acquaintances. But in this campaign, hundreds of families had put NDP signs on their own front lawns, balconies, and windows, and their neighbours had taken notice — in a good way. Then, all of a sudden, voters started to make up their minds. Within those twelve days our army of volunteers had identified seven thousand new supporters, bringing us precisely up to our target of nine thousand identified supporters. Now the challenge was to get them to vote.

A few days prior to the day of the vote in Outremont, who should call me but François Morris, my former bodyguard, who was now back with the service full-time. Catherine and I had remained in regular touch with him and his family. He would not be working on election day, he explained, and nothing would please him more than to drive me around on that crucial day. Needless to say, François, who is a man of very imposing stature, attracted quite a few quizzical looks as he escorted me around the riding.

That morning, our teams of NDP volunteers fanned out to ten "zone houses" across the riding to "pull the vote." They combed through their lists and ran door to door, but by late afternoon we had to face the fact that we had a serious problem. The data we were getting back from Elections Canada said our voters weren't turning out. My campaign manager Raymond Guardia, the NDP's national director of organization Heather Fraser, and national campaign adviser George Nakitsas took me out behind our campaign office in Mile End. They might as well have been taking me to the woodshed. We were going to lose, they warned. Despite an overwhelming grassroots campaign, despite, by all accounts, winning over the hearts and minds of the voters in the riding, our supporters had simply not turned up to vote.

I left the campaign office to go join my family, but insisted on coming back to see our core team before heading to the election-night gathering to thank our volunteers. It was only after I'd gone that the phones started ringing. Zone houses all over the riding were calling in, saying that voters they were speaking to at their doors, who we believed still had not voted, were insisting they had. It's not uncommon to have a handful of voters claim they've already voted even when they're not checked off on Elections Canada's lists, but this was hundreds. The data we were getting back from Elections Canada was being delayed to the point that it dramatically underestimated voter turnout.

When I returned to the campaign office it was pandemonium. The incredible team of young people we had assembled seemed like they were flying around the room. They had converted the phone bank into an incoming call centre, collecting the results coming in from dozens of polling stations across the riding; the numbers were slipped, shuffled, or shouted to volunteers at our bank of computers, who fed them into a system automatically displaying them at the election-night rally kilometres away. From there the results went to a giant board on the main office wall, where organizers compared them to a host of demographics and turnout targets. The room, in a word, was chaos.

As I walked in, Ray told me things were going better than expected. I tapped the shoulder of a young campaign staffer sitting at a computer, intending to ask him the latest results, but he was too focused to notice me. There were shouts back and forth from every corner. "We barely touched that polling area, and we just won it by five votes!" "We had twenty identified supporters in that poll, and just won with a hundred and five votes!" Their shouts grew louder. "We're not just going to win this thing. We're going to win it in a landslide!"

Watching this exceptional group of young people — we called them "the twenty-sevens" because no more than a couple were over thirty — shouting, yelling, laughing, screaming, celebrating, talking about their victory, about what *they* had accomplished, I have to admit I got a little emotional. My eyes started to well up. I snuck out the back door, into the same alley where a few hours earlier I'd received the news that my political career was finished. Quite the contrary. An entirely new chapter was just beginning.

In the end, the Liberals had been right to fear us for all those years, because not only did we win in Outremont by a margin of 4,441 votes over the Liberal candidate, but two-thirds of self-identified Bloc supporters voted for us. These were people who might have voted Yes in the last referendum because they wanted Québec to be respected in the Canadian federation, or else they were progressives for whom voting Conservative was not an option but who refused to vote for the scandal-ridden Liberals. Although very multicultural, Outremont is a majority francophone riding. French-speaking Québecers, including many passionate federalists, are rightly preoccupied with preserving their language, culture, and identity. My own great-grandfather, Honoré Mercier, who as a young man had been opposed to Québec entering Confederation, completely changed his mind once he saw that the rights of the *Canadiens-français* would be protected in the new country. The NDP as a party had long understood that many Québecers wanted nothing better than to continue as part of Canada, so long as their partners understood and respected their concerns. Now, twelve years after the 1995 referendum had brought the country to the brink of breakup, the voters in a francophone, nationalist riding dumped the Liberals and abandoned the Bloc, signalling their willingness to return to the Canadian conversation.

Our victory that day produced two very promising immediate outcomes. First, we'd shown that winning in Québec was possible, and second, we were now invited onto every political panel by the Québec media. All of a sudden we had visibility and we were punching well above our weight. From then on I received massive coverage, and very soon so did my leader, Jack Layton.

Once I was elected, Jack made me deputy leader along with Libby Davies and named me finance critic for the NDP. Jack and Libby took me out to Vancouver to spread the message that Québec was no longer a wasteland for the party. Closer to home, I travelled constantly across the province, making forays into the Eastern Townships, the Upper Laurentians, the Mauricie, Saguenay–Lac-Saint-Jean, and the Gaspé. Meanwhile, Mr. Harper's minority Conservatives were governing with the support of the Liberals, whose party was in disarray and loath to face another election.

Early in the winter of 2008 our party held a meeting in Montebello, Québec, and used the opportunity to signal that we would be voting against the budget unless the government took steps to immediately implement a $1 billion aid package it had announced for the forestry and manufacturing sectors. Why, asked Jack in his speech opening the meeting, had $14 billion worth of tax cuts been granted to immensely profitable corporations like the banks and the oil companies, at top speed and outside the normal budget process, whereas $1 billion of much-needed oxygen for Canadian cities with single-resource economies was taking forever to be released? Families were hurting because of policies favouring the rich brought in under Liberal and Conservative governments. "The Conservatives haven't done a thing for today's families or for the middle class," Jack continued. "In fact, they've made life less affordable for Canadians."

Sometime before that meeting we'd gotten wind through Pierre Ducasse, the president of the NDP Québec section, that the Liberals were manoeuvring to block Françoise Boivin as a candidate in the next election. Françoise had been the Liberal MP for Gatineau from 2004 to 2006, when she'd been defeated by the Bloc candidate. As a result, we'd called Françoise and invited her to come to the Montebello meeting. During our discussions with her she expressed great admiration for Ed Broadbent, with whom she'd sat on a parliamentary committee during her term in Parliament. It didn't take us long to get in touch with Ed, who was in England at the time, and to have him call Françoise to persuade her to run for the NDP.

Four by-elections had been called for September 8, one of them in the Montréal riding of Westmount–Ville-Marie. We had chosen a very strong, high-profile candidate to run in Westmount in the person of Anne Lagacé Dowson, a popular, impeccably bilingual CBC radio host in Montréal. About halfway through the campaign I got a call from an old friend in the provincial Liberal party in Québec City who asked me if I wanted to know what the federal Liberals' internal polls were saying about the riding Anne was running in. According to them, he said, she was two points behind the Liberals' star candidate, the former astronaut Marc Garneau. Our own polling said we were four points back, but we were developing a habit of closing strongly, so it looked like all bets were off in Westmount–Ville-Marie.

It was around that time that Stephen Harper, who was in the Maritimes, began musing aloud about Parliament becoming "ungovernable." We took it as a hint that he was thinking of calling a general election. The massive storm clouds forming on the economic horizon in the fall of that year were soon to burst, unleashing a financial whirlwind that would come close to destroying the world economy. Shortly before the by-election was to take place, Stephen Harper pulled the plug and called a snap general election, automatically overriding the by-elections. We ran a good campaign, and on October 14 I was re-elected, much to the surprise of the Liberals whose high-profile candidate was Sébastien Dhavernas, a well-known Québec actor. It was the first NDP victory in a general election in Québec in its entire history.

Even before that second victory, people's attitudes had begun to change from curiosity to readiness to take a serious look at the NDP. A few months before the election we held a meeting of the Québec section at the Hotel Rimouski, and we filled the place. Those were the first real signs that a wave was building out in the heartland beyond the confines of Montréal. Françoise Boivin, Guy Caron, Alexandre Boulerice, François Pilon, Jean Rousseau, Hoang Mai, Raymond Côté, Christine Moore, Anne-Marie Day, and Denis Blanchette, all of whom had run for us before, a few of them more than once, let us know they were willing to run in the next federal election. Today they are all members of Parliament.

Whereas in 2000 the NDP had garnered just 1.8 percent of the votes in the province, by 2006, under Jack's leadership, the NDP share of the Québec vote had risen to 8 percent. By 2008 we were into double digits, with 12 percent of the vote. And Québecers noticed. As time went on we were able to raise more money. We were able to hire organizers and hold events for cultural communities in Montréal. For example, we would have experts attend and hold a clinic on getting recognition for foreign diplomas and credentials. They were big meetings, with as many as two hundred participants. Jack often came to visit and was well liked in the province. Our message was strong and it was spreading.

Chapter Fourteen
Coalition Blues

On November 27, 2008, barely six weeks after the election, Stephen Harper's minority government, which had been re-elected with 37.65 percent of the vote while netting 143 seats in the House of Commons, tabled a fiscal update so wrong-headed and dangerous that the Opposition parties couldn't support it and were prepared to vote no confidence, even if it meant going back to the voters in a new election. The 2008 financial crisis had just brought the U.S. economy to its knees and threatened to collapse the world economy in the process. Major governments all over the planet were pouring millions into shoring up key economic sectors and trying to protect large numbers of average citizens who'd lost their jobs, whose home values had crashed, and whose savings had been wiped out. Action was needed and needed immediately. Yet here was our government announcing more cuts in government spending, along with a toxic mix of measures such as suspending civil servants' right to strike, making the historic fight for pay equity a non-starter, selling off Crown assets, and ending the government-funded per-vote financing that aimed to keep elections as fair and transparent as possible and helped to level the playing field between the parties. The Conservatives seemed clueless, paralyzed. Hundreds of thousands of jobs were being lost and they had nothing in their ideological tool box to help them to deal with the problem. But the Opposition parties, meaning the Liberals, the Bloc Québécois, and the NDP, having won seventy-seven, forty-nine, and thirty-seven seats respectively, held the majority of seats in the House of Commons with a total of 163 among us.

The complete absence of any stimulus measures to help prevent contagion from the economic meltdown south of the border and protect the livelihoods of thousands of Canadians spurred Jack to action. He called Ed Broadbent and asked him to contact former Liberal Prime Minister Jean Chrétien to explore the possibility of our two parties forming a coalition. There was ample precedent for such an arrangement. The British parliamentary system allows for coalitions. There are six examples of coalition government in British history, and coalitions have been formed in the past to govern provinces including Ontario, Manitoba, Saskatchewan, and British Columbia. More recently, during the short-lived Martin minority government, Jack, together with Mr. Harper himself, had co-signed a letter asking the governor general "to consult with the Opposition leaders and to consider all of [her] options," should the Liberal minority fall. Now, with the country in recession, as the Conservatives dithered and fumbled the ball, Jack initiated talks with the Liberals. It didn't go well at first, but the talks went ahead and a deal was struck. We in the NDP were willing to put a lot of water in our wine. Pledging to support the leader of another party as prime minister was the best proof of that. I was tasked with meeting with the Bloc to make sure that, after supporting the Conservative minority government time and time again, they would back a Liberal-NDP coalition budget. But there was electricity in the air. We did everything we could to keep the meetings secret, but the Conservatives were pouring massive resources into tracking our every move. It certainly was an interesting time. As a party, our priority was the best interest of the country, which, under the circumstances, meant getting rid of the Stephen Harper Conservatives. We would soon learn that the Liberals' priority was, as always, the Liberals.

The three parties agreed to ask the governor general to allow them to seek the confidence of the House in order to form a government. The

Bloc Québécois, which, though not a member of the coalition, held a balance of power in the re-elected Parliament, agreed to support it on matters of confidence.

As soon as the deal was known, Stephen Harper accused the Opposition parties of trying to overturn the result of the election, as if we were plotters in a palace coup instead of the parliamentarians elected by the vast majority of Canadians. At the same time, the Conservatives announced they would be moving up the date of the budget, which, instead of the planned spending cuts, would include an economic stimulus package. They also gave up on banning public servants' strikes and undertook to maintain the public financing of elections. The Liberals, loath to let the Conservatives snatch away their unhoped-for shot at retaking power, let it be known that they would use an Opposition day in the House to table a non-confidence motion and bring down the government.

Stephen Harper's reaction was unprecedented. He cancelled the Opposition day. Three weeks later, on a Sunday, as Catherine and I were attending a family get-together at my brother Sean's place in Saint-Lazare, I got an urgent message from Karl Bélanger informing me that the Conservatives had just made public a secret recording of a conference call between Jack and our entire caucus, during which he was heard to say, "This whole thing would not have happened if the moves hadn't been made with the Bloc to lock them in early, because you couldn't bring three people together as one in three hours. The first part was done a long time ago."

What had happened was that an email meant for our MP Linda Duncan had somehow been sent to Conservative MP John Duncan, who had a similar email address, and that the latter had surreptitiously joined in and recorded the entire call. Dimitri Soudas, the prime minister's press secretary, was going around handing out copies to the media, and PMO staff were distributing it electronically. Conservative operatives were out there spinning like crazy, portraying us as spineless interlopers who were prepared to do deals with traitors who wanted to destroy the country in their naked grab for power. They were demonizing the Bloc Québécois and us by association. The coalition was the *Bonhomme Sept Heures,* the bogeyman who was going to steal our cornflakes and make the sky fall, all rolled into one.

Jack and I, and our entire caucus, on the other hand, never lost sight of the fact that, whatever their views on the hypothetical future, Gilles Duceppe and our other Bloc Québécois colleagues were, until further notice, still our countrymen, just as all the Québecers who had voted for them were our fellow Canadians. This was totally consistent with the NDP's long-standing vision of the country, going back to Ed Broadbent and Tommy Douglas. Jack himself, during that leaked phone call, had expressed it well when he said that "nothing could be better for our country than to have the fifty members who've been elected to separate Québec actually helping to make Canada a better place." Needless to say, that part didn't get much coverage, probably because it didn't make for a sensational story.

In the meantime, Jack wanted me back in Ottawa ASAP to talk with media and deal with the storm. Even though our family had looked forward to spending a rare day together, I jumped in my car and headed back to Parliament to give a press conference and set the record straight. On the way there I made some phone calls. As far as I could tell, the Conservatives' dirty trick was not only shamelessly dishonest but probably also illegal under the Criminal Code. Despite it being Sunday, I managed to track down a lawyer colleague who was one of Canada's foremost experts on communications and media law. He walked me through the relevant Criminal Code provisions on capturing a phone conversation without authorization, and we later put in a request for the RCMP to launch an investigation.

In short order, the Conservatives launched a series of campaign-style attack ads, hammering the message that the coalition was antidemocratic and hinting darkly that we planned to seize power by nefarious means. The Prime Minister's Office marshalled a bunch of Conservative partisans to stage protests in the street outside Rideau Hall; the government announced that to hold onto power it would go over the heads of Parliament and if necessary of the governor general. Rather than allow a non-confidence vote to trigger the dissolution of Parliament, Stephen Harper resorted to ever more drastic action to keep himself in power.

Finally, on December 4, knowing he was headed for certain defeat in the House, Mr. Harper went for broke and presented himself at Rideau Hall to demand the prorogation of Parliament. There was an unprecedented public outcry. Less than two months after the election, Stephen Harper was shutting down Parliament.

After a lengthy meeting and a long vigil by the Ottawa press corps outside Rideau Hall, Governor General Michaëlle Jean gave Stephen Harper what he wanted. I have the greatest respect and admiration for Michaëlle Jean, who is now the secretary general of the *Organisation internationale de la Francophonie,* the worldwide organization representing countries where a significant proportion of the population is French speaking and that have a notable affiliation with French culture. (It is somewhat akin to the British Commonwealth.) She has never revealed the substance of her discussions with Mr. Harper. One can only hope that one day, perhaps in her memoirs, she will share with the nation what really happened. The result, in any event, was that Stephen Harper shut down the Commons, locking out the Canadian people's democratically elected representatives, in a naked attempt to hang on to power. Stephen Harper had lost the confidence of the House. Under convention, the governor general would ask for the leader of the Opposition to test whether he could have that confidence or if he or she had to call another election. Mr. Harper, afraid to face the House, shut it down to buy himself more time in the hopes that the coalition between the Liberals and the NDP would fall apart.

Of course the whole coalition-as-bogeyman Conservative scare tactic was a charade from beginning to end. Coalitions had ruled, quite successfully, in several Canadian provinces over the years, and less than two years later, in 2010, the United Kingdom would hold an election that would result in a coalition government. That coalition governed the United Kingdom for nearly five years, and no one ever deemed it undemocratic, illegal, or illegitimate.

One consequence of the parliamentary crisis was that the Liberal Party of Canada was thrown yet again into disarray. After the October election in which the Liberals had suffered a historic drop in voter support, Liberal leader Stéphane Dion had announced his intention to step down and remain as interim leader until the party could hold a leadership convention. For years the internal struggles between supporters of Jean Chrétien and Paul Martin had weakened the party and tarnished its brand as Canada's so-called natural governing party. Now, as the Conservatives pummelled Liberal leader Stéphane Dion, intoning that "losers don't get to form governments," the internal revolt brewing against the party leader burst into the open. On December 8, senior Liberals called for Dion's resignation, as Michael Ignatieff, who had made no secret of his ambitions and had a campaign organization up and running, very conspicuously waited in the wings. Dion was deposed, and on December 10, as soon as Ignatieff was installed as interim leader, the coalition began to unravel. Two days later, Michael Ignatieff and Stephen Harper met to discuss the budget.

On January 28, two days after the House resumed sitting, Ignatieff announced his party's support for the budget in spite of the fact that it still contained the very provisions his party had strenuously opposed only weeks before. Jack denounced the move, and our caucus voted against the government. From the time Mr. Ignatieff became the Liberal leader in December, his party supported the Harper government (either by voting with it or by abstaining) on every matter of confidence, ensuring that the legislation would pass and thereby avoiding an election for which the Liberals were not ready.

On the last day of August 2009, while Catherine and I were up at the cottage and everybody was on vacation, Michael Ignatieff travelled to Sudbury and, with his usual grandiosity, declared, "Mr. Harper, your time is up," before the assembled members of his caucus. The Liberals were signalling that they would no longer support the government. Take that, NDP! Perhaps they thought that this was a stroke of genius that would force us to get on the bandwagon or else stand accused of propping up the Harper government.

I spoke to Jack, who was in Halifax just finishing his vacation with Olivia. Jack and I had been exchanging emails in preparation for the fall session. The economy was still in recession, the country was bruised, and after barely averting a fourth general election in less than five years, voters were weary of the permanent campaign and the fervid atmosphere in Parliament. Jack and I agreed that what Canadians needed was a breather from all the political psychodrama and jockeying for power. We discussed Ignatieff's sortie and agreed that our party should refrain from bringing down the government as long as we could get concessions consistent with the principles the party had always stood for, and try to limit the damage from government policies to Canadian families as much as possible. We had done the same things under Paul Martin's minority government. As Jack was telling me that we should signal our intentions, my BlackBerry began to crash. I just had time to hear him say, "I'm off kayaking with Olivia, so you make the call," before I lost the connection. I stood there for a moment. I was deputy leader but it still felt a little like being thrown the keys to the car for the first time. I was alone at the cottage, so I wound up walking to the village to get to a pay phone and call a journalist to explain what we were going to do.

We abstained on a ways and means motion, and the government survived. We didn't support them. We used the balance of power jettisoned by the Liberals to benefit Canadians. That fall Mr. Harper agreed to one of our key demands and announced the government would invest $1 billion to extend unemployment insurance benefits to twenty weeks for long-term workers. It was good news for many families, it was good for the country, and it showed that we could responsibly influence government decisions to improve the lives of Canadians.

That Christmas, while Jack and Olivia were travelling abroad, Jack got unsettling news from his doctor in Toronto. He'd had some routine tests before leaving on holiday, and the results showed that he had prostate cancer. His doctor told him that he should begin treatment as soon as possible. Early in the New Year, Jack began treatment in Toronto. On February 5 he held a press conference in his riding of Toronto–Danforth. He had decided to go public. He felt a duty toward the thousands of men diagnosed with prostate cancer every year and was determined to give them and their families hope. With Olivia standing stoically behind him, he announced his condition to the nation. His father, who had been a Cabinet minister in the Progressive Conservative government of Prime Minister Brian Mulroney, had battled the same disease seventeen years before and recovered fully. Olivia, too, was a survivor, having been successfully treated for thyroid cancer five years earlier. Jack told the crowd of reporters that he was a fighter and that he was going to beat this, adding that he would remain as NDP leader and member of Parliament. Jack tackled the new session and his cancer with equal vigour and optimism. He was very open about his treatment.

Chapter Fifteen
La vague orange

W hen the New Year began we were putting the finishing touches on our plans for our most ambitious campaign in the party's history. We knew that the election could come as early as the spring, and we needed to be ready. Since becoming leader in 2003, Jack had kept his promise to make Québec a top priority. Brad Lavigne, who was national director of the NDP and had been at Jack's side when he'd made the promise, always made sure that our Québec team got all the resources we asked for as we built the organization and began recruiting candidates. Brad's bestselling book, *Building the Orange Wave*, gives a captivating account of all the hard work that went into implementing Jack's vision of what the NDP could achieve by bringing everybody together and completing the work of building the national party in every province. A brilliant strategist and tactician, Brad was our national campaign director in 2011 and is the senior campaign adviser for the 2015 election.

In the 2004, 2006, and 2008 federal election campaigns, the NDP had realized steady incremental growth, increasing its support from 1 million to 2.5 million votes and growing the caucus from thirteen to thirty-seven seats. Following the 2008 campaign, it was decided that it was time to cast the net wider than just a handful more seats. It was time to attempt a breakthrough campaign designed to ensure that the NDP was competitive everywhere in Canada, especially in Québec. To do so we required ground resources, a compelling message to take on the Conservatives, Bloc Québécois, and Liberals, and candidates who were worthy of voters' support. With a lot of hard work, we had all three.

In addition to the unprecedented resources for the Québec ground game, we spent a good deal of time carefully developing what our offer to Québec voters would be in the 2011 campaign. We knew from our constant touring of the regions that, overwhelmingly, Québec voters were looking for change in Ottawa. They wanted their federal government to grow the economy *and* protect the environment. They wanted Canada to be a voice of peace on the world stage. They wanted jobs and better retirement security. In short, they wanted change from Stephen Harper, and they couldn't get it from the Bloc or from the Liberals. Our offer, *Travaillons ensemble* (Let's work together), was an invitation for Québec voters who wanted change and had primarily voted for the Bloc in the past to work with other Canadians in the rest of the country who were also seeking progressive change in Ottawa. By uniting under the NDP banner in Québec and in the rest of Canada, we were saying, we can defeat Stephen Harper and build the Canada we want together.

In January I went up to Trois-Rivières for the nomination meeting of Robert Aubin, whom I'd recruited to run for the NDP. Robert was a teacher, the head of his union; he was articulate, personable, passionate. I had met him the previous fall at a conference held at the Université du Québec à Trois-Rivières (UQTR) to mobilize against the refurbishing of the now closed Gentilly-2 nuclear power plant, just across the river from Trois-Rivières. He was going to be an impressive candidate.

That evening he took us to the large bar complex where he regularly played in a band with a bunch of his friends. There I must have met at least 120 people, and every one of them told me they had always voted for the Bloc but now were going to be working for Robert's campaign as part of the NDP team. *That* was the first telling sign that our message was resonating. On the way home I called Raymond Guardia, who served as our Québec campaign director, and boldly predicted we were going to win in Trois-Rivières. Raymond didn't buy it. "Yeah, yeah," he said. I repeated the assertion, slowly this time. Raymond laughed. I could picture him rolling his eyes.

Not long before the start of the campaign, I went up to the Saguenay–Lac-Saint-Jean area to meet with our candidates and gauge the mood of the people there. Jack and I had done a swing through the region the previous year, visiting with workers at the aluminum plant run by Rio Tinto Alcan. This time I visited two Tim Hortons in Jonquière with candidate Claude Patry and a huge shopping mall called Place du Royaume in Chicoutimi with Dany Morin, an energetic young chiropractor who was our candidate in Chicoutimi–Le Fjord. We went in there at eleven in the morning, on a weekday, and spent two hours going store to store, stopping at every table in every coffee shop. Then people started pouring into the food court to have lunch and we went around, meeting and greeting every one. Pretty soon a TV camera showed up from the private network TVA, and that created a buzz. I must have shaken several hundred hands that day. I remember on the way home phoning Raymond again and saying simply, "Forty percent." "What are you talking about?" he said. "We're going to get 40 percent in Jonquière–Alma," I declared. In the end, we won there with 43.44 percent and in Chicoutimi–Le Fjord with 38 percent of the vote.

Just a few weeks later, in mid-February, Jack met with Stephen Harper and proposed a series of progressive measures that we wanted to see in the upcoming federal budget. We wanted action to lift every senior out of poverty and proposed an increase to the guaranteed income supplement (GIS); we wanted Canadians to save on their energy bills, so we proposed the removal of the GST from home heating; we wanted increased retirement security, so we proposed changes to the Canada and Québec Pension Plans; and we wanted to ensure relief for the millions of Canadians who don't have adequate access to health care, so we proposed investing in more family doctors. These plans were affordable and doable, and were part of Jack's offer to Canadians that the NDP was going be about "proposition as well as opposition."

Two weeks after that meeting with Stephen Harper, Jack underwent hip surgery without complications. He needed crutches, though, to get around Parliament Hill. Although he was in pain much of the time he didn't let his hip slow him down. Nor did the prospect of campaigning on crutches affect his view that if our proposals were not in the budget, the NDP caucus would be voting against the government and triggering the next election.

On March 21, the day before the tabling of the budget, the Standing Committee on Procedure and House Affairs, having repeatedly tried to get the government to release the estimated costs of its law-and-order agenda, tax cuts to corporations, and planned purchase of stealth fighter jets, produced a majority report recommending the government be found in contempt of Parliament. It was the committee's job to request the information, and the government's refusal was brazen, outrageous, and unprecedented.

The next day, Finance Minister Jim Flaherty presented his budget. After reading the highlights and conferring with me as finance critic and with NDP deputy finance critic Chris Charlton, Jack announced to the throngs of media in the foyer of the House of Commons that Stephen Harper had chosen to ignore our proposals and, as a result, the NDP would not be supporting the budget. Within days the Conservative government would fall on a motion of non-confidence and the election campaign would be underway.

We all took a deep breath. I went back to Québec where our NDP team had been busy for months, recruiting candidates, among them a group of really bright McGill students, several of whom I can remember driving home after NDP meetings. Whenever Jack came to Québec he campaigned flat out. He was spectacularly brave, radiating energy and optimism, and the sight of him campaigning, now with a cane instead of crutches, less than a month after his operation, drew people in and fired everybody up to work twice as hard.

I'll never forget a huge rally in Bloc Québécois leader Gilles Duceppe's own riding of Laurier–Sainte-Marie with 1,200 people. Jack's daughter Sarah, son-in-law Hugh Campbell, and granddaughter Beatrice had flown in with him on the campaign plane. Catherine and I met them in the green room of the Olympia Theatre as Jack was preparing to deliver his speech. But Jack was a lot less concerned with rehearsing than he was about fawning over his little granddaughter. Catherine and I have often reminisced about how Jack, despite his cane, despite the pain, kneeled down beside her, took her little hands, looked her in the eye, and said, "I'm doing this for you."

Jack would constantly remind us that what motivated him, particularly after the birth of Beatrice, was the responsibility he felt toward future

Making an announcement on protected areas at the Gault Nature Reserve, Mont Saint-Hilaire, with McGill vice-principal Morty Yalovsky.

At an evening gala with Catherine.

Speaking to the NDP convention in Québec City on September 9, 2006, a few months after my resignation as Québec's minister of the environment.

Jubilant former NDP leaders Ed Broadbent (right) and Alexa McDonough (in blue T-shirt) at our Outremont by-election victory celebration at Les Bobards in Montréal, September 17, 2007.

With Yvon Godin, NDP MP for Acadie–Bathurst at the Outremont by-election victory bash at Les Bobards in Montréal on September 17, 2007.

With NDP leader Jack Layton (centre) and Françoise Boivin (left) at the announcement that she would be running as an NDP candidate in the 2008 federal election.

With Brigitte Sansoucy (left), then national vice-president of the NDP, who ran several times for our party in Québec; Zahia El Masri (second from right), a party activist and former NDP candidate in Québec; and Alexandre Boulerice (right), a prominent member of the NDP who later became MP for Rosemont–La Petite-Patrie, after testifying on behalf of the NDP before the Bouchard-Taylor Commission on "reasonable accommodation" of minorities in Québec in 2008. The NDP was the only federalist party to do so.

With Jack Layton and locked-out employees of the Journal de Québec, *in Québec City, April 2008.*

Marching with locked-out employees of Le Journal de Montréal *on December 4, 2010.*

Addressing supporters at a campaign rally at the Olympia Theatre in Montréal on April 14, 2011, a few days before winning the May 2, 2011 general election.

With Jack Layton at the famous Schwartz's Delicatessen on Saint-Laurent Boulevard in Montréal, April 14, 2011.

With Jack Layton at La Cage aux Sports in Montréal, April 14, 2011.

My current deputy chief of staff, Chantale Turgeon, and my leadership campaign director, Raoul Gébert, during the NDP leadership convention in March 2012.

Sharing a hug with Catherine as we hear I have just been elected leader of the NDP at the Toronto Convention Centre on March 24, 2012.

Facing the media at the Toronto Convention Centre after winning the NDP leadership.

With Catherine at the 2014 Chinese New Year parade in Vancouver.

Getting a friendly greeting from local dog Bilbo in Whitehorse, Yukon, on March 11, 2014.

With the love of my life, Catherine, on board the ferry to Salt Spring Island, B.C., March 22, 2014.

Yukking it up with Mark Critch, host of CBC's This Hour Has 22 Minutes, *in Halifax, October 17, 2014.*

Catherine and her mom, Lydia, in July 2014, at the house in Aurillac, France, where a young Lydia lived in the attic for three years during the Second World War.

GLORIA VICTORIBVS

MCMXIIII
1914-1918

MCMXVIII
1939-1945

In my role as the MP for Outremont on Remembrance Day, with the Outremont war memorial in the background.

The Mulcair extended-family Christmas photo in 2014.

A March 2015 family portrait: Catherine, me, Greg, Catherine Hamé, Matt, grandson Raphaël, Jasmyne Coté, and granddaughter Juliette.

Meeting with Alberta's newly elected NDP Premier Rachel Notley on June 6, 2015.

generations. He summed up brilliantly his dogged determination to never let up: "Don't let them tell you it can't be done!" More than a slogan, it became our inspiration.

Prior to the campaign I had travelled to Sept-Îles in the riding of Manicouagan where Jonathan Genest-Jourdain, a young Innu lawyer from the Uashat reserve that is now part of Sept-Îles, was running for us. I met him in his community, at the Shaputuan museum, where his dad was one of the artists, and we went canvassing door to door. We worked the shopping mall, visited the offices of the band council, and held a press conference at which the chief spoke: "We don't endorse people in these campaigns," he said. Then he flashed a huge grin and bellowed, "But we couldn't be prouder that Jonathan is running!"

When I returned to Manicouagan during the campaign, a friend of Jonathan's told me a funny story. He'd volunteered to help Jonathan distribute the NDP signs for his campaign, but the signs had all been sent to Baie-Comeau, more than 230 kilometres south of Sept-Îles in the riding. This friend of Jonathan's was a plumber, and they set off in his truck to pick up the signs. On the way back they stopped to get gas in one of the first Innu villages along the coast. Some young guys approached the truck and, seeing the signs in the back with Jonathan's face on them, asked what they were. "I'm running," Jonathan answered. "You're running? One of ours? What do you mean?" Jonathan explained that he was a candidate in the upcoming election. They were gobsmacked and insisted he put up some signs on the spot. Young people are so connected, via Facebook and Twitter and all the other social media, that as Jonathan and his friend got to the second village a bunch of kids were waiting by the roadside to stop the truck because they also wanted signs in their community. By the time Jonathan and his friend had made their way back to Sept-Îles, a Facebook page had been created for him that already had hundreds of followers. When I came up the next day there were NDP signs up and down the roadside. What that said to me was that a community that had rarely ever voted in federal elections, the First Nations community in Manicouagan, a vast riding that extends along the St. Lawrence from Baie-Comeau to Blanc-Sablon and the border with Labrador and includes the island of Anticosti, was mobilizing to vote for our NDP candidate.

Up and down the province our people worked hard. Party stalwart Philip Toone, a respected notary who taught at the CÉGEP de la Gaspésie et des Îles and had been a long-time volunteer for the party, was running in the riding of Gaspésie–Îles-de-la-Madeleine. Guy Caron, an economist with the Communications, Energy and Paperworkers Union of Canada and former journalist who was the author of a report for the Council of Canadians titled *Crossing the Line: A Citizens' Inquiry on Canada-U.S. Relations,* was running for us again in his riding of Rimouski-Neigette–Témiscouata–Les Basques. Christine Moore, a francophone nurse from Abitibi who'd served with the Canadian Forces for three years and was a member of Nurses Without Borders, had run for us before and was now our candidate in Abitibi–Témiscamingue. Romeo Saganash, a former Deputy Grand Chief of the Grand Council of the Crees of James Bay and the first Cree to receive a law degree in the province of Québec, was the NDP candidate in the vast riding of Abitibi–Baie-James–Nunavik–Eeyou. Françoise Boivin, the lawyer and former Liberal MP who'd run for us in 2008, was running again. Françoise was extremely well liked in her riding of Gatineau, which had been a Liberal fortress since its creation except in the two previous elections, when the Bloc candidate had won. Nycole Turmel, a former president of the Public Service Alliance of Canada, was running for us in Hull–Aylmer, a Liberal stronghold in every election since 1917. In Montréal, Alexandre Boulerice, a prominent labour activist who'd run for us the last time, in 2008, was our candidate in Rosemont–La Petite-Patrie. Hélène Laverdière, a former Canadian diplomat who'd served in Washington, Senegal, and Chile, was running in Bloc Québécois leader Gilles Duceppe's fiefdom of Laurier–Sainte-Marie.

We knew something was really starting to happen. For the first time in our party's history we had a real Québec-wide campaign. As the Québec team of candidates were not big on meetings, we had only one weekly conference call to check in with all the candidates. I'll never forget the question put to us at the end of one call by Francine Raynault, who was running in the Bloc stronghold of Joliette held by Bloc House leader Pierre Paquette: "Why do you think the Bloc supporters are tearing down my signs?"

To anyone who has ever organized or been involved in an election campaign, having signs pulled down, though annoying and, indeed, illegal, is not unusual. What was big news here — and we all understood it immediately — was the fact that the Bloc would even bother to tear down our signs in a riding where, traditionally, the NDP didn't have much success. Despite the unprecedented investments in the NDP campaign, the Bloc still had much deeper pockets to invest in their ground game as well as voter identification and polling. They had begun to notice what we were picking up on the doorsteps, and they were lashing out. After the call, Raymond Guardia and I spoke privately. "Wow," he said, "they must really be seeing something that's making them nervous!" The stridency of Bloc attacks on Jack, me, and the NDP increased in the final weeks of the campaign. We were going to pull off something big, and they knew it.

We had many young high-quality candidates. Many of them, like nineteen-year-old Pierre-Luc Dusseault in Sherbrooke and the "McGill Four" — Charmaine Borg in Terrebonne–Blainville, Laurin Liu in Rivière-des-Mille-Îles, Mylène Freeman in Argenteuil–Papineau–Mirabel, and Matthew Dubé in Chambly–Borduas — were very young, energetic, and fluently bilingual. Others were accomplished professionals already making their mark on society. Pierre Nantel, a former musical artistic director with the Cirque du Soleil, and TVA and Radio-Canada columnist, was running in Longueuil–Pierre-Boucher; Hoang Mai, a young notary with a graduate degree in international law, who was the son of Vietnamese parents, was our candidate in Brossard–La Prairie; Anne Minh-Thu Quach, also with Vietnamese parents, a teacher and union activist, was running for the party in Beauharnois–Salaberry; Djaouida Sellah, who had been a volunteer doctor for the Red Crescent before immigrating to Canada from Algeria and was president of the *Association québécoise des médecins diplômés hors Canada et États-Unis,* supporting the recognition of qualifications of foreign-trained doctors, was running in Saint-Bruno–Saint-Hubert.

On May 2, election night, the scene at the Théâtre Rialto on Park Avenue in my riding of Outremont was complete pandemonium. Back in 2007 and 2008, my team and I had celebrated winning in Outremont at a bar called Les Bobards that we'd taken to calling our *"bar-fétiche,"* on Saint-Laurent Boulevard, a stone's throw from where Rebecca Blaikie and her *"colocs"* cohorts toiled in the tiny apartment that served as NDP headquarters. So I'd just presumed we would be going there again. But Raymond, who kept his eyes on the ground game on a daily basis, knew it would never hold the crowd he was expecting to turn out on election night.

When Catherine and I arrived at the Rialto with Greg, Matt, Jasmyne, and Juliette, our two-and-a-half-year-old granddaughter, we couldn't believe our eyes. A huge crowd, probably more than a thousand ecstatic, wildly cheering people, was pressed up between the stage and the exits in the lovely, ornate former movie theatre. But the massive presence of camera crews, reporters, and photographers from dozens of local, regional, and national media outlets in both official languages showed that this was real. It was all a bit intimidating for our little Juliette, so we made our way to the green room backstage, along with Mylène Freeman, who'd just been elected in the riding of Argenteuil–Papineau–Mirabel, and her mom, who'd driven in from her home in Ontario for the occasion. As the results rolled in from riding after riding, the crowd roared again and again.

We were in constant touch with Jack and Olivia in Toronto. The results in Québec were far from the whole story that night. As the ballots were counted across the country, there were NDP breakthroughs in ridings across Canada that either hadn't elected the NDP in a generation or — in many cases — ever. In the end, 4.6 million Canadians elected 103 NDP members of Parliament to form the largest Official Opposition since 1980. Even if you took away all of the seats gained in Québec that night, it was the best showing for the NDP in its fifty-year history.

The Orange Wave was the realization of much of the plan that Jack had laid out at dinner that November 2006 night in Hudson, when he'd turned to me and said, "That's where you come in," and had given me the chance to build that future with him. I could remember walking out of Jean Charest's office and packing boxes with Graham Carpenter at the riding office, not knowing if I'd ever run again, and I realized what a turning point in my life meeting Jack had been. Now it had all come down to this night, when Québecers in huge numbers had decided to place their trust in us.

When the media announced that the NDP would be forming the Official Opposition in Parliament, Jack and I spoke again, and the quiet joy in his voice brought tears to my eyes. A huge part of his vision was now realized. The chance to form a truly progressive government that reflected the values of all Canadians was finally within reach.

Chapter Sixteen
The Best of Times, the Worst of Times

On June 2, one month after the election, the House of Commons returned for a new session of Parliament. Jack had appointed Vancouver East MP Libby Davies and me to serve as deputy leaders. We watched with tremendous pride as our returning and new caucus colleagues marched into the House to occupy the Official Opposition benches directly across from Stephen Harper and his government caucus. Job one for us as the new Official Opposition was to hold the government to account. The second job was to show Canadians that we were the "government in waiting." That meant proving that we had what it takes to run the government of a G7 country. We could remind the nation that NDP governments had been in power multiple times in five provinces (now six, with Alberta) and one territory. We could quote from a study by the federal Finance Department stating that the NDP had the best track record of any party for balanced budgets. We could emphasize our proven reputation as good public administrators — under Tommy Douglas, Allan Blakeney, Roy Romanow, and Lorne Calvert in Saskatchewan; Mike Harcourt in British Columbia; Ed Schreyer, Howard Pawley, Gary Doer, and Greg Selinger in Manitoba; Darrell Dexter in Nova Scotia; and Tony Penikett and Piers McDonald in Yukon. Besides all this evidence, we were determined to show Canadians that as a federal caucus we had the experience, the competence, and the discipline to be trusted with governing the country.

Jack appointed me NDP House leader, a huge honour that made me responsible for the party's day-to-day business in the House of Commons and for negotiating with the government on matters pertaining to Bills and votes. Jack also put me in charge of bringing our new Québec MPs up to speed on parliamentary procedure and showing them the ropes around the precinct. The re-elected incumbents in the caucus, many of whom had worked for years on the breakthrough in Québec, couldn't have been more proud to welcome their new colleagues and helped them in every way they could. MPs from across Canada, including Paul Dewar, Charlie Angus, Peter Julian, Montréal-born Jean Crowder, Alex Atamanenko, Carol Hughes, Niki Ashton, Joe Comartin, Nathan Cullen, Megan Leslie, and Peggy Nash, most of whom spoke good French, and others who were themselves French-speaking, like Yvon Godin, Claude Gravelle and Denise Savoie, all became mentors to the new Québec MPs. We had a wonderful linguistic mix, and while some of our Québecers needed to improve their English, other members of our caucus whose French needed improving seized on the opportunity to upgrade their skills. I named Steve Moran as my chief of staff to help me in my new task. On broader issues he shared Jack's view, which I also embraced, that as a party we had to reach beyond our traditional base to all progressives, nationwide.

On that first day of the new session, the Canadian Union of Postal Workers (CUPW), which had been without a contract since January 31, 2011, initiated a rotating job action beginning in Winnipeg to inform the public about the refusal of their employer, Canada Post, to continue negotiating a new collective agreement. Although the job action was perfectly legal, the government accused the postal workers of undermining economic stability. The union offered to suspend their job action if the employer returned to the bargaining table and the old agreement was made to apply until a new one could be reached. But the Conservatives, bolstered by their new majority government, had other ideas.

On June 14, Canada Post locked out its workers, disrupting postal service across the country. One week later, Labour Minister Lisa Raitt tabled provocative legislation that ordered the postal workers back to work and forced them to accept lower wages than what the employer had last offered, an unnecessary, harsh, and punitive measure that showed the Harper government in a petty and vindictive light.

The Conservatives believed that with their majority in Parliament, they could ram the legislation through before the scheduled recess of the House on June 23. We had other plans. We decided to filibuster the Bill (a parliamentary tactic that consists of using every legal means at your disposal to delay the passage of a Bill, including talking and using procedural measures to keep the House in session around the clock) in hopes of forcing the government to come to its senses and let the employer and the employees go back to the negotiating table. Jack, who had lost weight during the gruelling thirty-seven-day election campaign and was visibly exhausted, led the filibuster. It was very hard on him, more than any of us could imagine. That day he rose in the House and gave one of the most magnificent speeches on workers' rights that I have ever heard. It was delivered with passion and purpose. Jack said: "Let us be clear, this bill [to end the lockout and impose a contract] violates the rights of workers to negotiate a collective agreement in good faith. It also weakens the collective bargaining rights of all 33 million Canadians; their right to work together with their co-workers to secure better conditions, a right entrenched in section 2 of the Charter of Rights and Freedoms…. This legislation sends a message to employers across the country that the government is prepared to side with employers against employees every time it has the opportunity to do so."

After he sat down he turned to me, and, as I leaned in to listen to what he wanted to say, I put my hand on his back. It was soaking. Jack said, "I'm feeling a little discomfort. Will you be able to give the wrap-up of the speech?"

"Sure, Jack," I said.

"And could you scrum after it's all done?"

"Of course," I said.

That was the first time he'd even hinted that something was amiss. Jack never complained, never said a word about himself other than that everything was going well, everything was going to be fine. He was extraordinarily stoic, in the noblest sense. He felt such a duty toward those workers whose collective bargaining rights were being trampled, and to all the others who would soon be in the government's sights if the legislation passed and set such a troubling precedent. All that day and right through the night, our entire caucus, especially the new Québec MPs, did Jack, our party, and their constituents proud. They gave wonderful maiden speeches on the importance of free and fair bargaining. Rookie NDP MPs were squaring off with seasoned veteran Conservatives just weeks after being elected for the first time. There was tremendous camaraderie among the entire caucus. There we were in the trenches, taking on the Conservatives on such an important issue. The team began to gel right then and there. If there was any doubt as to whether the new NDP MPs could handle the pressure of being parliamentarians … it was put to rest during that filibuster.

In the end the government used its majority to pass its destructive legislation, and with that, Parliament rose for the summer. Tired but exhilarated, it was time to catch my breath and recharge my batteries for the long four years ahead before the next election in 2015. I went back to Québec, and Catherine and I headed up to the cottage.

I love long swims and had been gone for a couple of hours on the lake before I got back and heard from Catherine that people were desperately trying to get in touch with me. Graham Carpenter had even sent his stepfather around to our house to deliver an urgent message. I phoned Jack's chief of staff, Anne McGrath, who passed me to Jack. His voice was weaker than I'd ever heard it. "I'm not doing well," he said. "I'm going to step down temporarily to concentrate full-time on my health and propose Nycole Turmel as a good person to serve as interim leader." I didn't realize it at the time, but with hindsight what he was doing is now clear. By choosing someone with solid experience and proven ability, whom he knew wasn't going to be seeking the leadership if the need arose, he was thinking ahead and providing for the future. To me, and to those of us who weren't at his side through his ordeal, it was unthinkable that he might leave us.

Catherine and I drove to my mom's place nearby to watch the press conference on television. When I saw Jack's flushed face and heard his raspy voice, I became very, very concerned.

The caucus gathered in Ottawa and held a meeting to confirm the choice of Nycole as the interim leader. Over the next couple of weeks I would write

Jack an email every few days to see how he was doing and to let him know we were thinking of him. On August 8, *"Nous sommes avec toi"* ("We're with you"), read the subject line. *"Salut Jack. Juste un petit mot pour dire que Catherine et moi pensons fort à toi. Ton courage et ta détermination nous inspirent tous"* ("Hi, Jack. Simply wanted to tell you that Catherine and I are with you in spirit. Your courage and determination inspire us all").

The one time he didn't write back, when I had passed along the best wishes of a mutual friend, I was quite concerned.

On Monday, August 22, Chantale Turgeon called me very early in the morning to tell me she'd just received two phone calls from journalists wanting to confirm that Jack Layton had died. I reacted with complete and utter disbelief. It wasn't possible. Such questions didn't deserve a response.

Then we started getting more calls in quick succession and messages on our BlackBerrys, all saying that Jack had passed away. I was just stunned. I couldn't believe it. Losing Jack, the leader who'd welcomed me into the family, who had enabled me to find a political home where people mattered and principles were valued, a friend and mentor who'd taught me so much about reaching out to adversaries and building consensus where none seemed possible, the *compagnon d'armes* with whom I'd stood shoulder to shoulder in Parliament for four years, the sunny, kind, fun-loving life and soul of our caucus — losing our indispensable Jack was simply inconceivable.

Catherine and I looked at each other, as the same thought struck us like a bolt of lightning. Olivia. Olivia was everything to Jack, and he to her. The bond between them was as vital and profound as the one we shared with one another. The thought of one going through life bereft of the other was unimaginable.

Catherine and I soon began to make plans to be with our political family in this time of gut-wrenching loss. Coming from such a big family myself, I know how important it is to be together at such a time.

On learning of Jack's death, the whole country went into mourning. The outpouring of grief from every part of the country was unprecedented. Thousands of Canadians came to pay their respects to Jack as he lay in state in the foyer of the House of Commons, and two days later at City Hall in Toronto. Tributes poured in from all over Canada. Others were carefully written or drawn in chalk, covering the pavement in Nathan Phillips Square outside Toronto City Hall where Jack and Olivia had served as city councillors for many years. The rains came and the messages were washed away, but the next day swarms of people were back on the square, many of them quoting from Jack's final message to Canadians: "My friends, love is better than anger. Hope is better than fear. Optimism is better than despair. So let us be loving, hopeful and optimistic. And we'll change the world."

On August 27 Jack was given a state funeral, after Prime Minister Harper, using his discretion as head of government, graciously offered him and Olivia the honour normally reserved for prime ministers and governors general. The ceremony was held at Roy Thomson Hall in Toronto and broadcast nationwide on most of the networks. It was heartbreaking.

Chapter Seventeen
A Test Unwelcome

For weeks we were all in a state of shock. Jack had been a lifelong friend to many in the party, a father figure to our youngest members, a teacher to us all. Our party was traumatized and hurting, with the distressing ordeal of choosing a new leader looming over us, robbing us of the time and space we needed to mourn and heal. Leadership campaigns are always perilous for any party, even at the best of times, because the wounds that can be opened are sometimes hard to heal after the race is over. The Liberal Party of Canada, which had just gone through four leaders in less than ten years, were ample proof of this. But for us in the NDP family, undergoing such a contest at such a painful time — with the media and the other parties posing as judge and jury — was an especially unwelcomed burden. For the previous three years, ever since our attempt at coalition with the other Opposition parties, the Harper Conservatives had used the Bloc as a bogeyman to sow division and distrust between Québecers and Canadians outside the province. Inflaming national discord wasn't beyond the Conservative playbook. Over the summer until Jack's death there had been speculation in the English-speaking media likening our newcomers from Québec to some sort of fifth column, a nationalist Trojan horse that was going to cause the NDP grief, just as

Brian Mulroney's Québec caucus had done to Progressive Conservatives. In such an atmosphere, whoever ended up replacing Jack was going to have to manage these and other false perceptions that the other parties were happy to spread about the NDP.

On September 12, Brian Topp, who had been elected president of the party at the convention in June and had been very close to Jack, announced that he was running. Brian had deep roots in the party, having at various times served as national campaign director of the federal party and as deputy chief of staff to Premier Roy Romanow of Saskatchewan. (In May 2015 he was appointed chief of staff to Alberta Premier Rachel Notley.) Along with Olivia and Anne McGrath, he had been at Jack's bedside as he lay dying and had helped Jack to draft his final message to Canadians. Brian had the support of Ed Broadbent, the party's beloved elder. It was a sign that some in the party wanted the leadership matter decided as quickly as possible. Ed's support gave Brian an advantage right out of the gate, and for other candidates, if any decided to run, the road ahead wasn't going to be easy. As for me, I didn't know what I wanted. Emotions were still so raw. Like everyone else, I wasn't over losing Jack. I needed to take the time to carefully consider what I should do in light of what was best for the party, what made sense for me and my family, and what I wanted to do for my country.

Then on September 16, four days after Brian, a second candidate announced. It was Romeo Saganash, who was now our star MP for Abitibi–Baie-James–Nunavik–Eeyou in northern Québec. Romeo was enormously respected. A skilled and experienced negotiator, he'd helped negotiate the *Paix des Braves,* the agreement signed in 2002 between the James Bay Cree and the province of Québec that redefined the relationship between them on a nation-to-nation basis. His was an outstanding candidacy.

Next, on September 30, Nathan Cullen, the MP for Skeena–Bulkley Valley in British Columbia, announced he was running. Nathan was an expert in conflict resolution and had been entrusted by Jack with several portfolios in the shadow Cabinet, notably environment, natural resources, and energy. He was in favour of joint nominations among non-Conservative parties in Conservative-held ridings to unite the vote around the candidate with the best chance of ousting the Conservative incumbent. On October 2 another top-notch candidate, Paul Dewar, the MP for Ottawa Centre who was the NDP foreign affairs critic, threw his hat in the ring, as did Martin Singh, who was president of the Sackville–Eastern Shore NDP riding association and president of the party's Faith and Social Justice Commission.

As we have always done, Catherine, Matt, Greg, and I sat down and put our heads together. We now also benefited from having Matt's wonderful wife Jasmyne join the family circle — she was a fantastic support, every step of the way. Choosing whether to seek the leadership was a huge decision to make. These were not normal times, and we understood that to many long-time members of the party I was still a relative newcomer. There were also personal considerations, of course. We knew the campaign would be a massive strain on the family. But, more broadly, Jack and I had worked tirelessly for nearly five years to bring Québecers to support the NDP and its generous vision of a society where no one is left behind. The Québec breakthrough that Jack had envisioned had now taken place and we were the Official Opposition, the precondition Jack had foreseen to forming the first national NDP government in Canada's history. Deciding whether I wanted to run for the leadership of the party therefore ultimately carried with it the decision of whether I was ready to run for prime minister.

I thought about how, in a country as diverse as ours, where communities with different histories, different linguistic and cultural identities, are separated by vast distances, it takes enormous effort, determination, and goodwill to bring everyone together. At the same time, I knew in my heart that Canadians were ready to put forty years of national acrimony and growing inequality under successive Liberal and Conservative governments behind them and to start building a more hopeful future. What was needed was leadership that could act as a bridge between Canadians, such as the one we had been building with Jack before he passed away.

As a Cabinet minister I had first-hand experience with the difficult decisions that government has to make, day in and day out, and I'd seen the difference that those decisions can make in people's lives. I believed that I could use my passion, training, and experience to help make life better for millions of Canadians; to fix the damage that the Harper Conservatives were doing to the country; above all, to call on all Canadians to work together and build the Canada of our dreams.

I remembered the advice that our sons Matt and Greg had given me when I was deciding whether to accept Jack's invitation to run for the NDP: to take a chance on the party that embodied the values instilled in me by the examples of my parents, of Father Cox, and of Claude Ryan and to help carry forward the vision imparted to me by Jack one November evening.

In the end we concluded that there was more to contribute. A lot more — and I was ready. With Geoffrey Chambers, Alain Gaul, Raoul Gébert, Chantale Turgeon, and Christian Leblanc, another friend and colleague, I assembled my campaign team, many of whom had contributed so much to my first federal election victory in Outremont. Raoul Gébert would be my campaign director. Long-time close advisers Graham Carpenter and Mathilde Rogue also played a central role. Ian Gillespie would be in charge of our key messaging.

We mapped out our campaign strategy: first and foremost, run a clean and positive campaign, from start to finish, no matter how things went for us; argue for broadening the base by signing up new members in Québec and reaching out to progressives across the country; focus on my experience in public administration and in government, as a manager, MNA, and Cabinet minister; make it very clear that if I were elected leader we would be working flat out to replace Stephen Harper and to form the first national NDP government in Canadian history, a truly progressive government that finally reflected our values and the values of all Canadians.

My team went above and beyond the call of duty in every sense, because we all recognized that the NDP now had an unprecedented opportunity to persuade Canadians to break the habit of always electing the same old parties that had ruled Canada for a hundred and fifty years and had so often disappointed them. This time the voters would be offered a clear choice for positive change.

Catherine took a leave of absence from her highly demanding career for six months, and on October 13 I announced that I would be a candidate for the leadership of our party. I launched my campaign in my riding of Outremont, in the big community centre at 6767 Côte des Neiges. Our two sparkling presidents of the NDP youth section for Québec, Catherine Hamé and Eddy Perez, introduced me in four languages. Looking out over the crowd that had come out to support me, with thirty-three of our NDP MPs by my side, one of my biggest surprises was spotting Denis Carrier, who had been my boss at the Québec Justice Department in 1978. He had driven down from Québec City and was just standing unobtrusively amongst the crowd, smiling. Seeing him brought tears to my eyes. When I went over to speak to him, he said, "I just wanted to wish you well. Let you know we're all on your side and want to help you in any way we can." It was an incredibly moving moment for me.

The NDP has a proud tradition of women in leadership, dating back to Thérèse Casgrain who was leader of the CCF in Québec from 1951 to 1957 and the first woman to hold a leadership position in a political party in Canada. Audrey McLaughlin was Canada's first woman to lead a federal party with representation in the House of Commons, from 1989 to 1995. But to date no woman had declared her intention of joining the race. Many people were urging Peggy Nash, our MP for Parkdale–High Park, to run. Peggy was an outstanding candidate, a former Canadian Auto Workers negotiator, and fluently bilingual. She launched her campaign on October 28. Two days later, on October 30, Robert Chisholm, our MP for Dartmouth–Cole Harbour and the former leader of the Nova Scotia NDP who'd come within one seat of forming the government in his home province, announced his candidacy. Finally, on November 7 Niki Ashton, the dynamic, multilingual young MP for Churchill in Northern Manitoba who'd so charmed the Greek voters in my riding, threw her hat in the ring.

As that exceptionally trying, momentous year drew to a close, Catherine and I enjoyed our thirty-six-hour Christmas holiday with the whole family at the cottage. Then I began travelling non-stop, as often as possible with Catherine, to every part of our vast country. Campaigns cost money, and ours was a shoestring operation from start to finish. I was billeted in supporters' homes from Kamloops to Halifax and treated to home-cooked meals by wonderful hosts, some of whom had welcomed Jack in the same way during his leadership campaign. Their warmth and encouragement were my fuel and inspiration for the tough slog ahead. The pace was gruelling, but the people we met gave me the energy and confidence to carry on through to the end. Many were people who'd stuck with the party through thick and thin, who'd carried the flame through the leanest years, and for whom the NDP was a party of principle. People who'd watched Tommy Douglas stand up in Parliament in October 1970 and, with tremendous courage, defend a fundamental principle of all free and democratic countries in stating, "We are not prepared to use the preservation of law and order as a smokescreen to destroy the liberties and freedoms of the people of Canada," before voting against Pierre Trudeau's War Measures Act. People who knew their history and who knew that so much of what Canadians cherish and consider part of their birthright — universal health care, unemployment insurance, pensions, old age security, public housing, … the list goes on — had all been conceived by, advocated for, or road-tested by provincial NDP governments. Most of all, this is what I was told by the people I met: *This time, we want to win.*

One of the more interesting political developments of the leadership race, very early in the New Year, was watching Stephen Harper invite himself into the campaign. On January 16 the media reported that I held dual French and Canadian citizenship. The Conservatives immediately seized on the issue, just as they had in the cases of Stéphane Dion when he'd been elected leader of the Liberal Party and of Michaëlle Jean when she'd been named governor general, both of whom also held dual French and Canadian citizenship. Somehow the issue had never come up in the case of Canada's seventeenth prime minister, John Turner, who held dual British and Canadian citizenship. But those were different times, and Mr. Turner's opponents were a different breed of Conservatives.

In my own case, Mr. Harper's interference was troubling on two counts: first, it was unseemly for the leader of a political party — let alone a sitting prime minister — to interfere in another party's leadership race. It just is never done, period. The bigger problem was with what he said and the message it conveyed. "I am very clear. I am a Canadian and only a Canadian," was a very unsubtle way of questioning my allegiance, and it sent out a disturbing message to the 863,000 Canadians who (at the time) held dual citizenship, many of whom had been born abroad and had actively chosen a better life in Canada. As for me, in earlier years I had never considered acquiring French citizenship. While Catherine and the kids held Canadian and French passports, I didn't, and that was that. I changed my mind twenty-five years ago, after border controls within Europe were relaxed considerably. On a trip to Spain with Catherine and the kids to meet up with her family for the Christmas holidays, we arrived at the Madrid airport to the usual holiday crowd. As in every other European airport, people holding a European passport were processed separately from foreign citizens. Noticing that there was a huge lineup for foreign passport holders and very few people in the queue reserved for Europeans, I encouraged Catherine to change lines together with the boys and have a hot chocolate on the other side while they waited for me to come and join them. As I stood there alone, it really troubled me that my travel documents weren't the same as my wife and children's. Catherine and I discussed it later, and although in the past she'd never insisted, she'd always thought it important for her to share her French identity with me, just as I shared my Canadian one with her. When we returned to Canada I applied for my French passport, which I proudly hold to this day. That said, as I stated in a television interview moments after winning my party's leadership, it stands to reason that as prime minister I will renounce my French citizenship, as did Michaëlle Jean in 2005 upon becoming governor general.

After the New Year things began coming together for my campaign. As I travelled across the country, I kept remembering what Jack had told me during the dinner in Hudson, five years earlier, about first becoming the Official Opposition if we wanted one day to form the government. That had been his near-term goal and he had achieved it brilliantly, before passing the torch that one of us was now going to have to grasp. If the party chose me to lead them forward, then it would be to complete Jack's vision and finally give Canadians a government that genuinely reflected their values and that responded to their needs.

On February 9, Romeo Saganash announced he was withdrawing his candidacy and throwing his support behind my campaign. Then on February 29, Robert Chisholm, who had withdrawn as a candidate in December, citing his lack of fluency in French, endorsed me, followed on March 14 by Martin Singh, who remained in the race but said that I was his second choice. Thirty-three members of our caucus had been at my side right from the start. As the weeks passed, current and past provincial premiers, including Ed Schreyer of Manitoba (former governor general of Canada), Mike Harcourt of British Columbia, and Piers McDonald of Yukon, declared their support, along with present and former leaders of the NDP in the provinces, former NDP MPs, present and past provincial legislators, municipal councillors, past and present labour leaders, and three labour organizations representing some of the most vulnerable workers in the country — the Retail, Wholesale and Department Store Union (RWDSU), the Service Employees International Union (SEIU), and the United Food and Commercial Workers (UFCW). We were beginning to show real momentum.

In the overheated atmosphere of leadership campaigns, the rumour mill goes into overdrive, fed by supporters of competing camps. This one was no exception. My history as a member of the Québec Liberal Party was predictably raised as an issue in an attempt to question my progressive credentials. There was just one problem. Many new party members were Québecers who'd joined the NDP during the Orange Wave, many of them progressive former Liberals whom we'd finally freed to vote with their convictions. We had decided early on that, no matter what was thrown at me, I would not respond. I wanted to wage a positive campaign.

My team and I stuck to that plan. All leadership candidates, regardless of political party, are faced with the same dilemma: if you attack your opponents, you can inflict lasting damage internally while at the same time handing your opponents in other parties ammunition to be used against you later. The Liberal Party of Canada had suffered from both, and we were going to learn from their mistakes. I knew that leadership races often turn ugly, although this was the first one I'd participated in, since both Québec premiers under whom I'd served had been chosen by acclamation. But Rebecca Blaikie, who was now president of our party and remained rigorously impartial throughout the race, had seen it all before. Rebecca is the daughter of Bill Blaikie, who had been the MP for Elmwood–Transcona in Manitoba for twenty-four years when he ran for the NDP leadership in 2003. And Chantale Turgeon, whose quiet insight I have relied on ever since my days as Québec minister of the environment, was always there to remind me of my pledge never to reply to negativity and always remain positive.

By March 23, the first day of the convention, which was being held at the Metro Toronto Convention Centre, my team knew we had a real shot at winning. Of course, Matt, Jasmyne, three-year-old Juliette, and Greg were there with Catherine and me for the convention. That night we celebrated Greg's thirtieth birthday with a wonderful family supper at the CN Tower. All through the weekend, our little granddaughter Juliette had a ball, soaking everything up and adding her own helpful advice. We had a team of young volunteers making campaign buttons. Juliette, like all inquisitive three-year-olds, asked them how the machine worked. Then she just joined in and spent hours punching out buttons by the dozen. At crucial moments during the weekend I headed to a curtained-off area of our campaign HQ to hold closed meetings with my key campaign advisers — Raoul Gébert, Chantale Turgeon, Geoffrey Chambers, Alain Gaul, and, of course, my family. Once, when she saw us all go in, Juliette briefly popped her head behind the curtain, looked around, and left without a word. Thirty seconds later a volunteer arrived carrying a chair, followed by Juliette. She'd looked inside, seen that there was no chair for her, and simply gone and commandeered one of the volunteers to carry a chair in for her. We cracked up as she joined the meeting.

The next day party members voted, on site and online from coast to coast to coast. There were problems in the electronic voting system that led to what seemed like interminable delays between ballots. My supporters spent hours in the stands cheering themselves hoarse with a phalanx of cameras trained on them, but with victory now so close, their energy never waned. At one point, just prior to the final round, as Catherine and I stood waiting in the wings, there suddenly appeared, at the top of a bank of cameras and journalists with their media equipment, the wide smile of my old high-school buddy Bob DiTomasso, who'd been one of the participants in our trip to Europe with Father Cox. He'd come in from Québec but later told me he'd been having trouble getting closer to where he might catch our eye, so he plunked down a chair just behind the journalists and climbed on to it so that he could see us. Only his head was visible, and when Catherine and I spotted him he was grinning from ear to ear. He made us all laugh out loud, providing comic relief at just the right time in those very long proceedings.

In the final crunch, after three ballots, Brian Topp, Nathan Cullen, and I were the only three left standing. I was elected on the fourth ballot. Brian came second, and Nathan came a strong third. We have some touching photos taken during my acceptance speech showing my sister Deb, who'd flown in from B.C. to help all weekend, patiently taking care of Juliette, who was getting restless and decided to seek greener pastures. In the end I was elected with support from every region of the country.

As it is with any newly elected leader, the first priority was to get the party ready for the next election. The first step in that task was to unite the party.

Chapter Eighteen
Leader of the Official Opposition

My first priority was to assemble my team. Each of the MPs who had run in the leadership race had exceptional skills and experience. I named them to key positions reflecting their importance to me as their leader and to the future of the party. Nathan Cullen became House leader, Peggy Nash our shadow minister on finance, Niki Ashton on status of women, Paul Dewar on foreign affairs, Romeo Saganash on international development, and Robert Chisholm on fisheries.

Typically in the British parliamentary system, the Official Opposition has two jobs: to hold the sitting government to account and to showcase its team of MPs as a government in waiting. On the first count, we quickly presented Stephen Harper with the first principled, structured Opposition he and his party had faced since taking power in 2006. As for the other part of the job, our caucus was filled with very strong people. They worked hard in their ridings and distinguished themselves in Parliament time and time again. The principled stands we took often made the evening news. The public got to know us, and the depth and competence of our NDP team was regularly on display.

We had a lot to get done. The people that help me and the NDP caucus carry out our responsibilities as parliamentarians are vitally important, and their skill, experience, and insight are essential. I asked Anne McGrath to stay on as my interim chief of staff. Anne had been a pillar of strength to Jack and Olivia, and to all of us, through the tragic days that had so closely followed the 2011 election. I valued her steady-handed professionalism, her deep experience in the party, and the far-sighted vision she shared with Jack. Like him, Anne had grown up in Québec and was fluently bilingual. She had studied at the University of Alberta and had lived in the West. Above all, Anne is a listener, with a unique ability to bring people together. Despite what had been an extraordinarily trying year for her, she agreed to carry on while Raoul Gébert completed his Ph.D. at the Université de Montréal, having postponed it to direct my leadership campaign. After he obtained his doctorate and received a prestigious award from the hands of the late Jacques Parizeau for submitting the best economic thesis of the year, Raoul replaced Anne, who took her immense talents to the private sector for a couple of years. I was able to persuade her to come back to the party she loves full-time as we prepared for a rendezvous with history in the next campaign.

Chantale Turgeon, the trusted adviser and confidante who'd been with me through so much of my political career, became deputy chief of staff responsible for my Parliament Hill office, for the tour team that arranges my cross-Canada travels, and for Stornoway, the official residence of the leader of the Opposition. Karl Bélanger, who'd been Jack's press secretary, had served with unerring political flair as a key member of the Official Opposition leader's team. I asked him to stay on as my principal secretary. Steve Moran, who'd been my chief of staff during my stint as House leader, would round out the senior team as deputy chief of staff responsible for policy and legislation.

For press secretary I turned to George Smith, whom I'd first noticed during the 2008 campaign and again in 2011 among the team of bright young people working flat out in our office on Avenue Papineau in Montréal, after we graduated from the *"coloc"* office on Saint-Laurent. Later, in 2012, I saw him at work again during the leadership race as a party volunteer in charge of logistics and media. I asked him to be my press secretary, executive assistant, and number one sidekick in Ottawa and everywhere I go across Canada.

There are many others whom I could name. The office of the leader of the Official Opposition employs over two hundred people, all of whom work long hours and give their all in support of our efforts. With my core team now assembled, we got down to business — and business there was, right from the start.

Every Wednesday, when our caucus met, our MPs returned from their ridings with stories of what government policies were doing to people out in the country. Families that had always thought of themselves as middle class were struggling to get by, and many other Canadians were juggling two, sometimes three jobs to make ends meet. Incomes were dropping and more and more households were going deeply into debt just to maintain their standard of living. Too many young families just starting out couldn't find affordable, quality child care. Tuition fees and debt were at an all-time high. Jobs were being lost, and the new ones being created were increasingly part-time and precarious. Fewer and fewer Canadians had the possibility of contributing to a workplace-based pension. The gap between the wealthiest few and the rest of the Canadian population was turning into a chasm. Canadians were hurting, and we were listening.

To that end, I began travelling as often as possible to every part of Canada. Right after I was elected leader in March 2012, Catherine, who for twenty-five years had been working in long-term and palliative care facilities in some of the poorest parts of Montréal, reduced from four to two the number of days she worked in the hospitals and kept one day of private practice so that she could accompany me in my travels across Canada.

One of the most important trips we took was a listening tour in the summer of 2013, heading into the 250th anniversary of the 1763 Royal Proclamation. The Royal Proclamation issued by King George III is a foundational document that is covered in section 35 of the 1982 Canadian Constitution, on the rights of Aboriginal peoples. The Proclamation established the Crown's fiduciary responsibility toward First Peoples. It even uses the word "nations" in referring to them. That summer, at every stop we made as we visited First Nations, Métis, and Inuit communities across the country, we met with and listened to the people. Few Canadians have the opportunity, as we did, to meet and speak to indigenous people in their daily lives. It is a humbling experience. It makes you realize just how huge the problems are and how their complexion changes from province to province. In British Columbia, very few First Nations have signed treaties, whereas other regions of Canada are almost entirely covered by treaty. In Québec, in the years following the James Bay and Northern Québec Agreement, the Québec government has worked tirelessly to develop a respectful nation-to-nation approach, the kind that is needed to transform the relationship between Canada and the indigenous peoples. The tour culminated in October 2013 with a reception that Catherine and I held at Stornoway with many of the indigenous leaders we'd met along the way.

On the eve of the publication of the Truth and Reconciliation Commission's report, Justice Murray Sinclair, the chair of the Commission, sat down with me at Stornoway to share the commissioners' findings and recommendations. On June 2, 2015, I was honoured to be present as the Commission made its report public. As I listened to Co-Commissioner Marie Wilson describe the harm inflicted on seven generations of First Nations children in residential schools across the country for more than a century, I thought about those kids I saw on the street in Winnipeg some thirty years earlier. I thought of my friend Romeo Saganash, who was himself sent to residential school as a child, and whose brother was one of the system's six thousand known victims. And I remembered the words the Honourable Justice René Dussault said to me, twenty years before, regarding the conclusions of the Royal Commission Report on Aboriginal Peoples that he and George Erasmus had worked on for three years: *This has to be fixed.* All that is lacking is courage and will.

Another major fact-finding trip we took, in early 2014, was what we called a "kitchen table tour," a tip of the hat to Jack, who during the 2011 campaign often reminded us: "Don't just listen to what's being said at the boardroom table, listen to what people are saying around the kitchen table." One of our first stops was in the riding of Laurentides–Labelle in the Upper Laurentians, where I met with a couple of retirees who had both been forced to return to work part-time in local fast food outlets, because their pensions simply did not provide them with enough to live on. She was in her late sixties, he was in his early seventies, and both had worked hard their entire lives. Now they were each putting in twenty hours a week just to pay the monthly bills. And their plight wasn't unique. Our MPs were reporting back from across the country with stories of seniors who were being forced into precarious, low-paying jobs just to make ends meet.

A little later, in Sault Ste. Marie, in Northern Ontario, we sat at the kitchen table of a young husband and wife, both of whom had recently completed their university studies. Both held master's degrees and, like many of their generation, they were starting out building their own careers. While I had every confidence they would each do fine, I was appalled to learn that they were carrying a crippling $130,000 debt in student loans, which they'd been paying off for years and would be for the foreseeable future. When, I asked myself, is a young couple loaded down at the outset with that much debt supposed to be able to start a family? These were the same young people who, when they became parents, would be required to pay up to $2,000 a month per child for child care. And their situation was not unusual. Today's young people who want to further their education and make the decision to put their earning power on hold in order to pursue it end up at graduation owing the banks the equivalent of a first home mortgage. Their families will likely spend their most productive years barely treading water, and they will reach retirement without enough to live on.

I'll always remember being in a union hall in Sudbury in February 2015. There I met a woman who said something that really moved me, as so often happens when you listen to people tell you their story. "I always just assumed that things would get better," she said, "but in fact they're getting worse." That's not right in a country like Canada.

We continued bringing those issues back to the House of Commons and holding the Conservative government to account. Parliament is often a raucous, hostile environment. Battles are waged there that impact Canadians right where they live on a daily basis. But there are times when everything changes. I'll never forget April 10, 2014, the day we learned that Jim Flaherty, the Conservative finance minister for nearly a decade, had passed away. Jim's resignation from Cabinet three weeks earlier, before tabling his tenth budget, had caught everyone by surprise. Health reasons had been invoked but taken with a grain of salt in the media, as these things often are. Jim had once been a tough, partisan, no-holds-barred politician when he'd served in Ontario Premier Mike Harris's government, but that wasn't the Jim Flaherty I knew. From the day in 2006 when he arrived in Ottawa as the member of Parliament for Whitby–Oshawa, Jim did his best to put his divisive partisan days behind him. He succeeded, winning the respect and friendship of people from all parties, on both sides of the aisle. When the surprising news began to trickle in that paramedics had been called to the home of the now former finance minister, my staff and I were up on the fourth floor, in 409S, the suite of offices and conference rooms assigned to the leader of the Official Opposition. As Parliament was sitting, my team and I were in the middle of our preparations for that day's Question Period. Mere minutes passed between the moment when we first heard that Jim might be taken to hospital and the official confirmation that he had died. As the distressing news spread through the halls of Parliament, it was immediately obvious that neither I nor the rest of my team were going to subject our Conservative colleagues to the kind of tough, rigorous questioning that we had become known for.

Strangely, there is no device of parliamentary procedure allowing to simply cancel Question Period. As the expression of the people's will in a functioning democracy, it automatically overrides all other considerations. But not this day. It just wasn't going to happen. "We cannot do QP today," I told my team. "I'm going to talk to Speaker Scheer." There was an immediate sigh of relief from the half-dozen staffers who had been drafting some of our questions. I took the stairs leading to the back door into the House of Commons. Along the way I offered condolences to the stunned Conservative colleagues I met as I passed the door to their side of the House. I quickly went into the Speaker's chambers and said to Andrew Scheer, "We can't do this today." His expression was one of shock, very quickly followed by relief.

To their credit, even while reeling from the loss of such a close and dear friend, the government side had not entertained the possibility of trying to cancel Question Period. Not only because of the central role Question Period plays in our democracy, but because the government was under fire for its highly controversial electoral reform legislation and couldn't be seen as evading questions. The request to cancel had to come from the other side of the House. The Speaker said he would immediately consult with the Conservative House leader, and thanked me sincerely as I left his office.

From there I headed into the Opposition lobby to talk to our Liberal and Independent colleagues. The same grief-stricken atmosphere reigned on our side of the Chamber, where people had already begun reminiscing and telling stories about Jim. As I entered the House, the prime minister gestured to thank me. We met in the centre aisle and spoke briefly. I expressed my condolences to him personally and on behalf of my party. He'd shown himself to be extremely decent when Jack had passed away, and his decision to give our leader a state funeral had been a classy, noble gesture.

The Speaker rose, called the House to order, and then asked for and was granted unanimous consent for there to be no Question Period that day. Afterward, MPs milled about in the House for quite some time. There was a kind of shell-shocked camaraderie that brought back memories of the time around Jack's passing, when gestures of kindness had been made that won't be soon forgotten. At times like these Parliament is at its best.

Then there are events that bring the whole country to a standstill. The first inkling we got of one such tragedy was on October 20, 2014, when we heard that two members of the Canadian Forces had been run down by an unknown assailant in a shopping centre parking lot in Saint-Jean-sur-Richelieu, Québec. That afternoon, before any details began to trickle out about the victims or the perpetrator of the crime, Randy Hoback, a Conservative backbencher, rose in the House to ask a scripted question of his own government, invoking "unconfirmed reports of a possible terror attack against two Canadian Forces members near Saint-Jean-sur-Richelieu" and asking the prime minister to update the House on this matter. By then, one of the victims, Warrant Officer Patrice Vincent, had just died of his injuries. We soon learned that the perpetrator, Martin Couture-Rouleau, who'd been killed by police, was a *pure-laine* francophone Québecer. That fact didn't fit with the narrative the government had immediately put out, about "the international jihad" at work in Canada. It didn't seem to matter that the killer had been a deeply troubled young Canadian who, having suffered a serious personal setback, had become obsessed with terrorist websites and claimed to have converted to Islam. Nor was it deemed relevant that his family had become concerned about his mental health and tried in vain to get him professional help, and that the RCMP had had the young man under surveillance for some time. What mattered was that, in the wake of this tragedy, Stephen Harper could invoke the word "terrorism" and unsettle the nation, before the investigation into Warrant Officer Patrice Vincent's murder had even begun.

Two days later, on the morning of October 22, 2014, our caucus held its weekly meeting in room 253D, otherwise known as the Railway Room, on the ground floor of the Centre Block on Parliament Hill. The officers of caucus, including myself, the whip, and the House leader, sit at a table on a riser facing our colleagues, with a clear view of the main doors of the room, which open onto the corridor. Suddenly there was a loud bang somewhere outside, and Alain Gervais, one of the security guards, came in, shutting the door and pressing his back against it as if to block the entry. There were several more loud bangs, like someone whacking two garbage can lids together. Having sat through noisy protests by groups trying to get into meetings at the *Assemblée nationale*, I spontaneously took this to be a group of demonstrators trying to force their way into the government caucus room directly across the hallway. But our MPs from Northern Canada, who didn't need to be told what they were hearing, hit the floor immediately. That first loud volley of six or eight close, cannonading shots was followed by more shots further down the hall, toward the door at the far end of the corridor that marks the entrance to the Library of Parliament. Then began a crackle of small arms fire — dozens and dozens of shots — mixed with yelling, and finally quiet.

We were rushed out of the room by the same brave guard who'd stood against the door the whole time and led away down the hall to safety on the Senate side of the building. We were shown into a ground-floor location and told to keep below the line of sight of the room's many windows. Soon, the security forces came in and said they had orders to get me out and to take me somewhere safe. I declined and stayed with the caucus.

Thankfully, I was quickly able to reassure Catherine, Matt, and Greg. While my colleagues reached out to their loved ones as well, my first concern was for the safety of those of our MPs who weren't in the room with us and for my staff, who had remained upstairs in 409S. It was a long time before I could ascertain that all were safe and accounted for, but with the help of the whip's office and our director of operations, Gisèle Dupuis, we managed to complete a head count. Gisèle deserves special mention as crisis manager for calming our staff, organizing rapid counselling sessions, and keeping everyone informed.

We spent the rest of the day in lockdown. MPs began giving interviews to reporters from local media in their constituencies. We were repeatedly told to get down on the floor, because there were reports of three, then five shooters on the roofs. These turned out to be false reports made by nervous people spotting security personnel. My staff four storeys upstairs in the office of the leader of the Opposition later recounted being escorted out by Special Forces members armed with machine guns and taken to a secure location, where they too were put in lockdown along with staffers from other parties.

As Opposition leader I had to keep my people focused, because we had work to do. Beyond the confines of Parliament, the country was frightened, anxious, and confused. We had a responsibility to reassure our fellow citizens that their democracy was intact, that their leaders were in control, and that our values as Canadians were unshakable. I got word to my staff to start drafting an address to the nation on behalf of the Official Opposition, to follow the one our prime minister would surely want to deliver that evening. Our young staffers worked with incredible dedication, under enormous stress, to develop the themes we had discussed together. Very late in the afternoon, on short notice, we got confirmation that I could give a televised speech if I wished to. I consulted with caucus, and my colleagues unanimously urged me to do so. My chief of staff, Raoul Gébert, and I were escorted out of the parliamentary precinct to the CBC building on Queen Street. Minutes later, Sparks and Queen Streets were again in lockdown. We had just managed to slip through. Press secretary Marc-André Viau handed me the final version of the speech. Earlier that day, he and his colleague Greta Levy had come within a few feet of the shooter, yet a short while later they were back on duty.

My address to the nation sought first and foremost to reassure Canadians. The attack, I said, had taken place on the very ground where we come together to exchange ideas, with the knowledge that, whatever our differences, we will always resolve them peacefully. Though intended to make us more fearful of our neighbours and less confident in ourselves, it had failed. Instead, it had succeeded only in drawing us closer together, in making us stronger. I praised the determination, professionalism, and heroism of the women and men of our law enforcement, our security services, and our Canadian Forces. Their acts of courage would remain an abiding emblem of Canadian values and valour. The thoughts and prayers of everyone in our nation's capital were with the family and loved ones of Corporal Nathan Cirillo — the Canadian Forces hero from Hamilton, Ontario, who had been standing on guard at a monument dedicated to the sacrifice of others who came before him when he lost his life that morning. Our thoughts were also with the loved ones of Warrant Officer Patrice Vincent, who'd been felled two days earlier, and with his injured colleague and his loved ones. Thirty-four million Canadians — at home and abroad, from coast to coast to coast and around the world — stood united, and we would not forget. We had been shaken, but we would not waver. We had woken that morning in a country blessed by love, diversity, and peace, and tomorrow we would do the same. The attack had been driven by hatred, and was designed to drive us to hate. We would not hate. We would stand up, and we would stand together. We would persevere, and we would prevail.

The funerals for Corporal Cirillo in Hamilton and Warrant Officer Vincent in Longueuil were some of the saddest events I've ever attended. Corporal Cirillo's extremely brave young son and Warrant Officer Vincent's twin sister stand out in my memory. Vincent's sister had just lost part of herself, and you felt it. Her eulogy was eloquent, dignified, and heartbreaking.

It was American President Franklin D. Roosevelt who famously said that "the only thing we have to fear is fear itself." Contrary to popular belief, he said it at the height of the Depression, in 1933, in his first inaugural address, six years before the start of the Second World War. In saying those words, he brought the American people together, harnessed his nation's energies, and, for the next decade through the Second World War, inspired Americans not only to achieve extraordinary economic and social progress, but to defend democracy at home and abroad.

At first, the day after the shooting, Prime Minister Harper seemed to rise to the occasion, as he stood in Parliament, reaching out to the Opposition and urging all Canadians to unite in response to the horrific attack. But the moment soon passed, and the Conservatives seized on the tragedy to invoke fear of "international jihadism." Stephen Harper himself called "violent jihadism" "one of the most dangerous enemies our world has ever faced" and warned against "the jihadist monster" whose "tentacles" supposedly reached into unsuspecting communities across the country. Where President Obama referred to "houses of worship" when talking about rooting out terrorist threats, Mr. Harper used the word "mosque," specifically. Even more shameful was the prime minister's deliberate conflation, in campaign-style events and in the House of Commons, of terms such as "Muslim," "Islamic," or "niqab" with hot-button words like "jihad," "terrorism," and "anti-women." It was wedge politics at its most egregious, cynically designed to divide Canadians, create suspicion where none existed, and dehumanize as "Other" those who were our neighbours, workmates, and colleagues — our fellow Canadians. When our prime minister singled out one community, one religion, and associated it with something as violent and frightening as terrorism, that was not leadership.

As I write these words, there are a million Muslims in Canada. Many are prominent members of our communities across the country. Many others, who have recently come to our country from afar, congregate in areas of our largest cities, like wave after wave of immigrants before them, including my own Irish forebears. Their children grow up loving hockey, poutine, Tim Hortons muffins, our national anthem, and our country — and all the while they keep, and share, their own cherished traditions As Ottawa journalist Stephen Maher, whose ancestors, like some of mine, came from Ireland, pointed out in a recent column, "Nobody talks about the Fenian threat these days" (*National Post,* February 21, 2015).

In the aftermath of the attack on Parliament, the Conservatives moved with unseemly haste to ram Bill C-51, their massive, draconian new national security legislation, through Parliament and invoked closure to cut off debate. Their behaviour was disturbingly reminiscent of the Bush administration's actions after 9/11, when they forced the 342-page Patriot Act on a shell-shocked Congress without giving legislators time to read it. Bill C-51 is a monstrosity, denounced not just by the NDP but by no fewer than four former prime ministers, five former Supreme Court judges, and scores of legal scholars from across the country. Its title alone gives the measure of its reach: *"An Act to enact the Security of Canada Information Sharing Act and the Secure Air Travel Act, to amend the Criminal Code, the Canadian Security Intelligence Service Act and the Immigration and Refugee Protection Act and to make related and consequential amendments to other Acts."* The worst of it is that, according to the Commissioner of the RCMP himself, none of the measures contained in the Act would have prevented the murder of Warrant Officer Vincent or of Corporal Nathan Cirillo. As for the Liberals, they said they didn't like it but would nevertheless vote for it because, in their leader's words, they were "months from an election campaign" and didn't want the Conservatives to "make hay" if they voted against the repugnant Bill.

The threat of international terrorism is serious and must be addressed with vigour, in a manner that respects the Charter of Rights and Freedoms and bedrock Canadian values. Legitimate dissent and civil disobedience, whether by First Nations, environmental groups, or anyone else, must never be targeted, as the current wording of the legislation very clearly does.

Chapter Nineteen
A Country Based on Shared Values

When my ancestors on my father's side fled their native Ireland, they were leaving behind a beloved land ravaged by a famine of historic proportions. In North America, at the time, two of the main ports of entry for the desperate Irish were Boston and Québec City. Many of the Irish immigrants whose descendants went on to settle in Montréal first came to Québec City, where in the early part of the twentieth century they joined the thriving French-speaking community. Today there is a beautiful Celtic cross at the foot of Saint-Stanislas Street with a commemorative plaque inscribed in French, English, and Gaelic, which reads: "To the people of Quebec from the people of Ireland in Remembrance of their selfless compassion in a time of need."

When you look at the history, you realize that there were diseases on board those ships, diseases that the people going down to the docks to help those poor and destitute Irish were inevitably exposed to. Many of Québec City's inhabitants actually died as a result of the diseases brought on the Famine Ships, yet the French-Canadians kept meeting the ships and taking in strangers, especially the many orphans whose ill and famished parents had perished during the crossing. Those children were encouraged to keep their Irish surnames, the better to remember where they came from. It's why many French-speaking Québecers have Irish names today. Those who went to the docks each time a ship came in, even knowing the risks involved, did so simply because there were people in distress arriving in their midst who needed help. Their compassion is emblematic of the openness and kindness with which this land has historically welcomed newcomers, from the earliest days when the indigenous nations came to the aid of the first settlers, among them my own maternal ancestor Julien Mercier, showing them how to build shelters and survive through the harsh winters, how to grow food in summer and recognize medicinal plants to heal common ailments.

In the history of Canada, it must be said, there have been episodes when we weren't so compassionate: when, in 1885, we imposed a head tax on Chinese immigrants and then in 1923 barred them altogether, after thousands had given their blood, sweat, tears, and, many, their very lives, to build our transcontinental railway; when, in 1914, the *Komagata Maru*, a chartered Japanese steamship carrying 376 Asian immigrants from the Punjab, most of them Sikhs, along with Hindus and Muslims, were denied landing in the port of Vancouver and sent back to India, where many died or were imprisoned; when, in 1939, 937 Jewish refugees fleeing Nazi Germany were turned away as they approached Halifax and sent back, 254 of them to die in Hitler's death camps; when, in 1941, all persons of Japanese heritage in Canada were removed from their homes and sent to internment camps. And there is our history of broken treaties and colonial domination over the indigenous peoples of this land. Nevertheless, Canada as a country has always returned to its founding principles of pluralism, tolerance, and solidarity — because we know we stray from those principles at our peril.

Canada was built on immigration. The famine-stricken Irish who came to these shores landed here with nothing but what they could carry. Many of those who moved on to Montréal settled in Griffintown, where they went to work in the factories of the city that was Canada's financial, industrial, commercial, manufacturing, and cultural hub for most of our country's history. They worked hard. They scraped for every penny. And their descendants are today among the leading figures of Montréal's business, academic, legal, medical, and artistic communities. The Irish experience is a familiar story and common to all of us whose ancestors came here from afar, from no matter what country of origin. It is the quintessential Canadian experience. Ours is a generous, open-hearted country, filled with honest, hard-working people whose families came to Canada believing this was a land where, if they worked hard, played by the rules, and lived within their means, they could make a better life for their children. People who valued fairness and social justice, democracy, equality, and human rights — and believed in them strongly enough to uproot themselves from the places they knew to start from scratch in a new land of wondrous possibility.

Everywhere Catherine and I travel across Canada, Canadians tell us they want change after years of hollow promises, scandals, and fear campaigns of one kind or another. Many things need fixing in this country — and we'll do more than talk about it. As Jack always said: "Don't let them tell you it can't be done!"

It's time to remember how strong we are when we work together. Much has been lost in recent years, but not the values and principles that made this country such a brave, bold experiment on the North American continent. One that eschewed violence as a means of resolving conflicts, in the belief that peace, order, and good government would provide the necessary conditions for dialogue and accommodation, and inevitably lead to a brighter future.

My vision for that brighter future is clear: a country whose government grows the economy and creates stable, full-time jobs, while protecting the environment; where our youth get the opportunities they need and our seniors get the benefits they deserve; where democratic traditions are respected at home and our reputation as a country is respected abroad; where fear and division are replaced with shared confidence and optimism.

I believe that every young family just starting out should have every opportunity to succeed, and that families that need access to quality, accessible child care should have it. Québec has had a publicly subsidized child-care system in place, staffed by licensed caregivers in regularly inspected facilities, for over fifteen years, and it has proved to be a tremendous success in allowing many more women to enter the labour market. I am proud to have been a member of the *Assemblée nationale* when that plan was brought in. It can be done. Parents in Quebec pay between seven dollars and thirty cents and twenty dollars a day per child for a place in a *centre de la petite enfance* (early childhood education centre). For many young couples with small children, life in Québec is much more affordable and sustainable.

I believe that access to affordable child care is an economic as well as a social priority. Kudos must go to the boards of trade and chambers of commerce across the country who have joined the NDP in working toward quality, affordable child care for Canadians in every province and territory. A national child-care program has been promised by every Conservative and Liberal government since 1984. Even Stephen Harper once promised to create 125,000 child-care spaces. Together, nine Canadian governments — five Conservative, four Liberal — have failed to deliver a single one. It's time to put an end to empty promises and to get the job done. The plan I have presented, fully mapped out and announced months before the election, will create one million $15-a-day maximum child-care spaces in every corner of Canada in the next ten years. We will create a system of quality, affordable child care that serves hard-pressed parents across Canada and respects the jurisdiction and specific needs of each of the provinces in which they live.

I believe that every Canadian should be able to retire in dignity with financial security. That is why we need to ensure that the Canada Pension Plan, which Canadians have paid into their whole lives, will be there for them when they turn sixty-five; that workers who've paid into a workplace pension aren't left with nothing if their employer goes bankrupt; and that all Canadian workers have a portable workplace pension that they can take with them when they change jobs.

I believe that a family with two children and both parents working full-time at minimum wage should not be living in poverty. The federal minimum wage was abolished almost twenty years ago by the Liberals, and the responsibility was left to provincial governments. That's a lack of leadership. The result has been that since then wages in general have stagnated, when they haven't fallen. Under an NDP government, that's going to change. We will bring in a minimum wage pegged at fifteen dollars an hour for workers under federal jurisdiction and that will be a signal for the provinces and territories. The best way to stimulate the economy is to put money in the hands of people who are going to spend it on goods and services. We will focus our efforts on creating conditions that will allow young people and working families in this country to aspire to a better life, instead of resigning themselves to expect less and less for themselves and their children. We want to build a society that provides good, stable jobs in the new economy of tomorrow.

As a grandfather, I don't want to leave an unfair environmental burden on my grandchildren — I believe we have an obligation to take responsibility today. Previous governments have failed to protect the environment, and the damage done is hurting our quality of life, our health, and our economy, and tarnishing our global reputation. Worst of all, it risks being our legacy to future generations. An NDP government will establish, in law, clear criteria for resource extraction and transportation based on the principles of sustainable development, which include internalizing all pollution costs and putting a price on carbon. In our day and age there is no longer any way around it. Any new energy project requires a thorough, credible environmental assessment process, based on criteria of sustainable development and social acceptability. We don't have one in Canada, because the Conservatives have gutted all the relevant existing legislation and reduced the staff responsible for enforcing it.

When I was the minister of the environment and of sustainable development in Québec City, we brought in overarching sustainable development legislation. It set out basic principles, such as polluter pay, that the government had to follow when creating policy or drafting legislation. We went so far as to amend the Québec Charter of Human Rights and Freedoms to include the right to live in a clean environment. It's had the effect of producing jurisprudence that communities now can rely on when challenging a project they deem dangerous or damaging to the environment. That's the type of vision we will bring to the federal scene.

In December 2015 a crucial international summit, the United Nations Conference on Climate Change, will be held in Paris, with representatives from every nation. Under an NDP government, Canada will cease to be seen as an international pariah on the vital issue of Earth's climate and join the community of nations striving to tackle the biggest challenge facing the world this century.

Climate change is a dire threat, factually and undeniably, and it's the heating of the Earth's atmosphere caused by human activity that drives it. As early as January 2004, less than a year after the U.S. invasion of Iraq, the

Pentagon issued a hair-raising national security threat-assessment forecast predicting that, twenty-five years on, the biggest danger to peace, security, and stability worldwide would not come from terrorism but from climate change, with large-scale floods caused by sea-level rise; mega-droughts desiccating major areas; wars over food, water, and energy resources; and masses of displaced people fleeing their countries to survive. And the issue was not new. I had become aware of the problem in the late 1980s when the World Meteorological Organization and the United Nations Environment Programme, at the request of U.N. member states, created the Intergovernmental Panel on Climate Change to bring together the research of climate scientists the world over. In 1992 the Earth Summit in Rio produced the first ever international climate treaty (the United Nations Framework Convention on Climate Change) and, although falling short of actually setting binding greenhouse gas emissions limits, it raised awareness of the issues in the broader public to an unprecedented extent. Five years later, in 1997, the Kyoto Protocol was added to the treaty, setting out green-house gas emissions reduction targets for member countries. The United States, however, never signed it, and it remained a toothless instrument, including in Canada where the governing Liberals, although talking a great game, admitted years later that they had no plan to meet Canada's obliga-tions. Stephen Harper reneged on Canada's signature, making us the only country in the world to have withdrawn from the Kyoto Protocol.

But there is worse. On November 16, 2010, the Conservatives used their majority in the Senate (which by then had been packed with the prime min-ister's hand-picked appointees, many of them defeated candidates) to over-turn historic climate change legislation that had been tabled in the House by the NDP and voted into law by a majority of members of Parliament. The law would have required the federal government to introduce regulations setting clear targets to reduce greenhouse gas emissions in Canada by 25 percent below 1990 levels by 2020 and to set long-term targets to bring emissions down 80 percent below 1990 levels by 2050. The Conservative senators struck down the legislation by calling a snap vote, without allowing any time for debate whatsoever. For the first time in seventy-five years the unelected Senate had brazenly defied the will of Parliament and of the democratically elected representatives of the majority of Canadians. Upon learning of the deed, Jack was more upset than I'd ever seen him. He had tears in his eyes as he met with reporters to denounce the move. The new law would have allowed Canada to show leadership on a vitally important issue for the world and its citizens. Instead, our country has continued to do worse than nothing on emissions.

Still the challenge remains, and it has grown even more urgent during the wasted years when our government and many others dragged their feet, putting at risk the future for all our children. When it comes to the Earth's climate, there isn't a moment to lose. Liberals and Conservatives alike have consistently enacted tax breaks — $50 billion worth of them to date — for Canada's largest, most profitable corporations, including oil companies. They both support the Keystone XL pipeline that even President Obama has been loath to approve. They are both committed to our antiquated fossil-fuel-based economic model, when so many countries are already beginning to reap huge economic rewards from their investments in innovative green energy technologies that will power the future world economy. Stephen Harper wants to leave these problems for our children and grandchildren. I won't.

More than anyone else, Catherine, her judgment and values, have guided everything I have tried to accomplish in my family life and in my career. I was also blessed to have such exceptional parents, and to have inspirations like Father Cox, Claude Ryan, and Jack Layton at key points in my life. My last conversation with Claude Ryan took place when I was Québec environment minister. He was very ill and passed away very soon after. He was kind and generous, as always, but also as determined and clear-eyed as ever. We both knew that he wasn't going to be with us for very much longer. After some personal exchanges, he said something that has guided me ever since, at every step of my career. "Monsieur Mulcair," he said, "we have to remember why we're elected. It's to help people."

I've always tried to live up to that entreaty. Father Cox, Monsieur Ryan, and Jack all believed passionately in the power of each of us, as individuals, to redress injustices, right wrongs, and make a difference in people's lives. They all had in common a core belief that the struggle and suffering of others make moral demands on us to help in every way we can. It isn't enough to talk about fixing what is broken in society. You have to mean it and mean it enough to actually do something about it. Whether it's seniors looking to make ends meet or young people preparing to start out in life, middle-class Canadians are struggling. But the plight of the poor and vulnerable is even more dire. Every year at Christmas time I lend a hand at Sun Youth, a respected and well-established community group in my riding of Outremont that was founded over fifty years ago by Sid Stevens. In recent years, Sid has explained to me that families requiring assistance are more and more often the working poor. Betty MacLeod, who has been a friend for decades and runs Agape, a wonderful Laval charity, and other community organizations, tells me that she sees the same every day. The cost of everything has gone up, but wages are low, and work is often part-time and precarious. Twenty-five years ago, a resolution was adopted unanimously by the House of Commons promising to eradicate child poverty. A quarter of a century later, one million children in our country are poor and go to bed hungry. I can't accept that this is inevitable in a country as rich and as generous as ours.

Under the decades-long watch of the two old parties, Canadians have had to settle for ever-diminishing expectations. In 2015, for the first time in 150 years, Canadians will have the opportunity to vote for the change they want and get a government that keeps its promise. Together, with the strength of our convictions, we will build for our children and grandchildren a good and decent Canada where all can prosper, and no one is left behind.

Index

Throughout the Index, Tom Mulcair is referred to as TM.